Performance Reviews, Empowered Careers

Titles in the CAREERSAVVY Series™

Performance Reviews, Empowered Careers

Ann Coil, Ph.D., and Ann Hult Crowell

Impact Publications
Manassas Park, VA

Library of Congress Cataloging-in-Publication-Data

Library of Congress Cataloguing-in-Publication Data

    Ann Coil
       Performance reviews, empowered careers: powerful communications that advance careers / Ann Coil, Ann Hult Crowell
         p. cm.
       Includes index.
       ISBN 1-57023-184-2   2002109079

Publisher: For information on Impact Publications, including current and forthcoming publications, authors, press kits, online bookstore, and submission requirements, visit our website: www.impactpublications.com.

Publicity/Rights: For information on publicity, author interviews, and subsidiary rights, contact the Media Relations Department: Tel. 703-361-7300, Fax 703-335-9486, or email: info@impactpublications.com.

Sales/Distribution: All bookstore sales are handled through Impact's trade distributor: National Book Network, 15200 NBN Way, Blue Ridge Summit, PA 17214, Tel. 1-800-462-6420. All other sales and distribution inquiries should be directed to the publisher: Sales Department, IMPACT PUBLICATIONS, 9104 Manassas Drive, Suite N, Manassas Park, VA 20111-5211, Tel. 703-361-7300, Fax 703-335-9486, or email: info@impactpublications.com.

Contents

Acknowledgments

We'd like to thank the following people for their help, ideas, suggestions, resources, and evaluation.

Mardie Younglof, our muse, who expertly guided us through the editing and proofing process with great skills, a sense of humor, and encouraging support.

Leslie Etheridge, a consummate human resources professional with a wealth of information about the performance appraisal process.

Diane Moos, a superb manager any employee would love to have as a boss and mentor who gave us the "manager's" view.

The clients of Ann Coil, who have taught her so much as she's guided them through their careers.

The employees and staff of Ann Crowell, who has learned the true meaning of "valued employees" by having the opportunity to lead and learn from a dynamic group of people.

Our families, friends, and colleagues, who provide constant inspiration and support.

Introduction

You just finished your annual performance review, so now you can relax for a year. Right? Wrong.

Performance review is an ongoing, cumulative process. Throughout the year, **even though you are unaware of it,** you are constantly communicating your value to others within the organization. Like an actor onstage, you should always be prepared, look smart, and behave appropriately vis-à-vis others in your cast.

Onstage and Prepared, Every Day

The annual performance review often takes center stage in people's minds as the primary mechanism for validating and advancing their career. Shift your focus from that dreaded ritual which takes place with you and your manager on opposite sides of the desk and, instead, think about the many opportunities to bring your career front and center throughout the year. Reflect on those relatively relaxed daily encounters in the hallway, at the coffee machine, or in the lunch line with managers, bosses, and co-workers. In every situation, you're on review as others consciously or unconsciously assess your appearance, personality, and behavior. Whether you like it or not, you're onstage every day. Your audience listens to what you say and evaluates you accordingly.

Prepare for Career Conversations

Today's fast paced, performance-oriented organizational world requires you to always be prepared for career-related conversations. Finesse in showcasing your talents reinforces your value to the organization and enhances your job security. With the rapid, unexpected changes in management as organizations shrink, re-organize, and merge, your boss today may not be your boss tomorrow. You may suddenly find yourself having to re-establish your credibility and value with a whole new set of players. Your ability to communicate your capabilities and achievements to the new management and get feedback on their goals, style, and priorities allows you to get up to speed fast and secure your future on the new team.

Our goal is to help you handle career conversations no matter where or with whom they take place:

- Chance encounters with your boss

- Networking opportunities with influential co-workers

- Feedback sessions

- Progress reports

- Meetings with a new team

- And the all-important performance review

In each of these situations you and your career are onstage! And each one of them will be more effective and successful if you're always prepared and primed to describe **what you are doing and your results** in a compelling, but tactful and gracious manner.

What Can You Get From This Book?

We start off with a crash course for those of you facing a performance review in the near future. The simple four-step preparation process will tame those pre-performance butterflies and make sure you are ready with your lines so you can convincingly communicate your accomplishments, report on your progress, underscore your value to your organization, and present your career goals.

After the crash course we'll coach you to take the big-picture view of your career and see it as an ongoing, masterful work-in-progress. We'll lead you through the important steps in the process so you can handle any and all types of career encounters throughout the year, including your next performance review. The following chapters show you how to:

❑ **Assemble and organize** for easy retrieval from your work history the basic information that you need to communicate in career conversations — your skills, talents, experiences, accomplishments, etc.

❑ **Identify** the factors that bring you career satisfaction to help you establish and communicate your career goals for the upcoming year and long term.

❑ **Keep informed** about your organization so you can determine and communicate to your boss how your efforts and talents contribute to its mission, goals, challenges, and priorities.

❑ **Investigate** career opportunities in your organization to determine if and where you want to move and how to relay that information to your manager formally or informally.

❑ **Thoroughly prepare** for a performance review.

❑ **Give** a great performance review.

❑ **Bounce back** if you receive a bad performance review.

❑ **Captivate** your audience by using engaging stories to communicate your skills, experiences, and accomplishments.

❑ **Handle** the important communication loop with your manager by learning how to give and get feedback.

This process helps you **sort out** the unidentified mass of things you do every day and then re-package them so you can see for yourself, and help others see, the countless contributions you make to your manager's and your company's success. You'll discover all the occasions where you influenced others, and learn how to present important aspects of yourself countless times a day.

Our goal is to make you comfortable and adept with this ongoing career process. Career-related conversations will be **integrated** into your "persona," easily and coherently expressed without being seen as continually **advertising or promoting** yourself. You won't need a crash course the next time your performance review rolls around!

1

The Performance Review: A Crash Course

Are you facing your performance review **soon** and feeling unprepared to go onstage? This crash course gives you the basics you need in order to present yourself effectively as you step into the spotlight. Later chapters help you prepare in more depth, but these quick tips are what you need **now** to get through that impending review.

Consider the basic purpose of the performance review. Forms and formats vary with each organization, but the information that performance appraisal systems are designed to elicit from employees is similar across all organizations. Basically, management wants to know:

1. The skills and knowledge you have as well as the skills and knowledge you need to improve or acquire.

2. The tasks and projects you have completed and to what degree you have met the goals and objectives set forth in your last performance review.

3. How you have grown or developed in your job and in your career.

4. The goals and objectives you have established in the coming year.

Do a credible job in handling these four performance areas, and your review will be a success—for you and your manager. The goal of this chapter is to help you do a good job under a tight deadline. Before you start this crash course, however, take a few moments to do some preliminary work that will make this whole process flow more quickly and smoothly. Like painting a room or preparing a big Thanksgiving day meal, gathering your tools and doing a little prep work **save** time, aggravation, and mistakes down the road.

Activities to Do First

1. **Read over** the performance review form and make sure you are clear about what the organization is asking, the definitions of terms, and the meaning of the rating scale categories included in the form.

2. **Assemble** documents that record and track your work history for the past year—tasks, projects, responsibilities, and results. These documents can be job notes, progress reports, your old performance review, a current resume (if you have one), memos from your boss or colleagues, or your calendar, or Day Timer, etc. They'll jog your memory about important past activities and results that now lie dormant in your mind, swept over and forgotten by a flood of new, more recent activities.

3. **Prep your manager.** If time permits, send your boss a bulleted list of your accomplishments, and link the information to the broader organizational goals.

4. **Examine** your last performance review, paying special attention to your goals and objectives. Be ready to discuss which goals and objectives you achieved and to what degree you achieved them. If you didn't achieve a goal, be ready to discuss why, what you are doing to make sure you do achieve the goal in the future, and the time line.

5. **Tune in** to the current key priorities of your organization. What are the organization's mission, goals, trends, challenges, and major initiatives? You'll need to link your skills, talents, and accomplishments to these organizational priorities.

With this preliminary work done, you're ready to tackle the four performance review areas.

Four Performance Areas

1. Skills and Knowledge

Best Skills—First, review the information you gathered about your work history, and from those activities identify and list your best skills and knowledge areas.

Link Skills to Priorities—Second, review your skills list and select the ones that make the best link to your organization's priorities, goals, challenges, trends, etc.

Skills or Knowledge to Improve or Acquire—Third, since performance reviews also focus on growth and development, identify and list the skills and/or knowledge areas you'd like to acquire or improve. Also, list suggestions how you might do this.

Scripts

Here are some ways to communicate your skills and knowledge areas.

> **Best skills:**
> *"My customer service skills are strong because I am good at defusing anger and getting to the person's issue or problem; I am excellent at follow-up and follow-through and get compliments from both co-workers and customers on these skills."*
>
> **Link to organizational priorities:**
> *"Our goal is to increase our customer base by 10%. My good customer service skills not only get new customers, but get more business from the customers we have."*
>
> **Skills or Knowledge to Improve or Acquire:**
> *"I could be more effective on the job if I increased my knowledge of our two latest products. Could I tour production or take one of the classes designed for the sales team?"*

2. Tasks, Projects, Responsibilities and Results

Using the documents you pulled together in the preparation phase, identify three to five of your best accomplishments. They could be major projects, specific assignments, an important responsibility, or a series of related tasks. Pick the ones that seem most significant and are most directly related to the organization's current goals or challenges.

Use this simple formula to describe your accomplishments to your manager:

Why the effort was necessary
(This will drive home the importance and value of your efforts.)

What you did
(Outline the actions you took and the skills you applied.)

The results you achieved
(This will describe how the organization benefited.)

Scripts

"I initiated tours of client facilities for our project manager to provide better client support and service."

Why the effort was necessary

"The environmental division of our firm was not getting enough repeat business, and we had too many problems and client complaints."

What you did

"As the business manager who worked with the project managers and fielded questions and problems from clients, I set up tours of client facilities for project managers so they could develop more rapport with our clients and more clearly assess and diagnose clients' environmental safety problems. I had to convince the managers that it was worthwhile and then take pains to schedule them at convenient times for both the managers and the client company."

Results achieved

"The project managers enjoyed the activity, once they got used to the idea, and felt more confident in their service to the clients. We doubled our repeat business from the prior year and cut our complaints by 70%."

3. How You've Grown in Your Job/Career

Demonstrating professional growth is an important part of a performance review, even if you are not planning to advance to a more responsible position. In today's volatile job market you can't afford to mark time. You **must** show that you are keeping your skills and knowledge current.

So, as you cram for your upcoming performance review, don't forget to discuss how you've improved, added, or honed your job-specific skills as well as your personal skills.

Scripts

On the job performance

"As I looked at our company's needs and the multiple business and office management roles I play, I felt the marketing role was becoming increasingly important for me. I took a class at the local university on marketing for technical professionals. I've gained a broader perspective about marketing and sales for technical organizations, and I see that relationship building and networking are

extremely important and can reap more benefits than advertising and direct mail. This was one reason I suggested the tours of clients' facilities, which have turned out to be an excellent marketing tactic for us."

Personal development / personal management / career development.

"I also took a career assessment class, which reinforced my interest and skill in marketing, particularly relationship building. This approach gives me the in-person and people-to-people work I enjoy."

4. Goals and Objectives You've Established for the Coming Year

Often you and your manager set your next year's goals together, but when you come to the performance review with your own ideas of what you want to accomplish in your work, you demonstrate initiative and resourcefulness. As you set your goals, remember to keep in mind the organization's most important needs and challenges direct your goals to those priorities as much as possible.

Script

"In addition to recruiting, I'd like to work on more training, particularly in the area of diversity. I'd like to minimize the work I do on training support. Joe, who is in training support, would like to expand his job, and I think he could pick up my extra work so I could focus on training, diversity, and recruiting. We have diversity in our strategic plan and mission statement, but no one person is taking responsibility for it. I would like to work into that position. I can continue to do my job in recruiting and have the satisfaction and excitement of working on a new project I believe in.

I have been reading and studying about diversity and recruiting. I've developed skills and knowledge through my interaction with the professional group. I already know the organization, the possibilities, and a lot of the players. I need your support and that of upper management to do this and assistance in setting appropriate goals for diversity. I'd also like to sit on a company-wide committee where diversity could be represented. Do you know of any such committee?"

When Time Is of the Essence

When preparing for any performance under a tight deadline, it's better to present a few things well, than to cover a variety of topics poorly. When cramming for a performance review, pick at least one topic from each of the four performance review areas and strive to present it well.

If it's possible given your manager's workload, schedule, attitude, and state of mind, ask for a postponement. However, if you do this, present a plausible (and true) explanation. You might say, for example, that you have found some guidelines to help you do a better job of preparing for the review and you'd like more time to utilize this resource.

Another possibility is to ask for a follow-up meeting. Since career goals are best handled in career conversations that are held separately from the performance review, ask for a follow-up meeting to discuss your career issues. This gives you more time to think through your goals and take advantage of the help provided in this book.

Just remember, the goal here is to demonstrate your value and commitment to your work. Keep this goal in mind, be tactful and sensitive to your manager's challenges and working style, and you can make this performance appraisal a win-win on short notice.

2

Preparing Your Story

Onstage? Know Your Lines

Have you ever dreamed you're in a play, don't have a script, and are feeling panicky? That's how it feels when you are unprepared for a performance review or an important meeting with your boss. You don't know what to say or how to say it!

Stage fright subsides, however, when you know what you want to say. Having lines slip fluidly from your tongue tames the butterflies and builds confidence, but to deliver this script flawlessly, you must work from a sound story line.

To deliver their lines convincingly, good actors do more than put on a costume and apply makeup. They "slip into the skin" of the person they are playing and transport themselves into the history, heart, and experience of the character. They "study the story" to learn the character's strengths and weaknesses and what drives his/her behavior.

To perform well in career conversations, you, too, must know **your** story—what makes you tick? What's your history with the organization? What value do you bring? What knowledge, skills, and experience do you possess? What strengths give you an advantage? What limitations do you need to address? The details of your story often get lost in the dizzying whirl of the workday merry-go-round. It's easy to take all you do for granted and "forget" to tell your manager or supervisor what you want them to hear:

- Problems you solve

- The customers you serve well

- The project you salvage

- Disasters you prevent

- Co-workers you help

- Money you save

- Revenue you generate

7

Instead of resorting to a crash course on the performance review, spend some time with this book and manage your career throughout the year. You'll find yourself in the director's chair, guiding your career wherever you want it to go. Because you know what you want and what you have to offer, the lines will flow easily and the performance review and other career conversations will be a breeze.

This Chapter as Your Coach

Actors have the advantage of a ready-made and scripted story line, character descriptions, and a director to guide the action. You, on the other hand, play **all** the roles—story editor, scriptwriter, director, and actor, with the sole responsibility for unearthing the golden nuggets of your experience in a compelling story that conveys your value, skills, and contributions.

We're here to coach you in your storytelling. In this chapter we help you excavate all the important and valuable things you've done for the organization, those things that fade from your memory over time, squeezed out by an onslaught of new activities. In Chapter 3 we show you how to pinpoint the organization's most important goals and link your efforts to those priorities.

Before you launch into your story we provide stage directions that make your storytelling easier.

Seven Kinds of Career Conversations—First, we describe seven different settings in which career conversations can take place. These settings, or types of career conversations, determine the purpose and content of your story.

Collection Section—Next we discuss how to set up a system to organize and easily retrieve the valuable information you'll be uncovering.

Your Story—This is the heart of the chapter. We coach you in sorting through the history of your work experience in order to uncover, reclaim, and record your numerous skills and accomplishments.

"Fast Save"—Finally we introduce you to *Fast Save*, the greatest thing since talkies. It's a quick, easy method to maintain an ongoing record of your work accomplishments. You'll have the most important information you need ready to deliver at a moment's notice.

So, spend a little time with us here. You won't be sorry. The work you do in this chapter will set the scene for any career conversations you hold in the future. You'll save angst and anxiety down the road when—whether it's a planned engagement or impromptu performance—you find yourself ONSTAGE!

Seven Types of Career Conversations

Basically, career conversations break down into seven categories, each with its own setting and purpose. Your work in this book helps you step into any of these situations and pull off a winning performance. The specific context, or type of career conversation you are having, will dictate what information you need to present and how you present it.

1. The Performance Review

The performance review is a formal, structured, and pre-planned event that has a great influence on your career now and in the future. Its purpose is to evaluate your performance against pre-determined objectives, to quantify your contribution to the organization, and set new objectives for the coming year.

Long before the actual review takes place, the organization is acting on important information and decisions that affect your future, such as promotion possibilities and compensation. Thus, it's in your best interest to start working on your performance review preparation three months in advance.

2. Career Conversations

Career development conversations focus on the management and development of your career—your needs, preferences, and goals. They are more open and free flowing than the performance review and address your development and growth rather than "evaluations" of past work efforts. Ideally, it is best to keep career conversations separate from the performance review because the "feeling of being judged" may inhibit the dialogue about career goals and preferences.

3. The Individual Development Plan (IDP)

The IDP can be separate from, or a part of, a performance review or career conversation. Your IDP details **how** you are going to achieve your career goals and objectives. It may include more education or training, new experiences, informal updating and polishing of skills and knowledge, regular meetings with your manager, and other formal and informal ways to work toward your goals and the organization's expectations of you. Taking charge and being creative in developing your own ideas for your career development will enhance your status in the company's eyes.

4. The Progress Report

Progress report encounters often don't come with the costumes and trappings of the formal performance review, but don't let their sometimes-casual disguise fool you. They are also important career scenes. You can look like a champ when you pull off a great project. You can look like a chump if you don't. However, you can rise above the ashes of a project going down in flames if you can communicate that you're doing a good job of problem-solving and putting out the fire.

5. Informal, Impromptu Boss-Encounters

Hallway encounters, discussions over lunch in the cafeteria, a conversation at the organization's picnic or holiday party, a chance meeting in the parking lot may just be casual, friendly opportunities to connect with your boss. They can also be golden opportunities to give unsolicited input and updates about tasks that are going well, accomplishments you achieved, and positive feedback you've gotten from co-workers or customers.

6. General Networking and Relationship Building

Why include general networking—non-boss encounters—in a book on career conversations and performance reviews? Because discussions you have while networking can be some of your most important career conversations. Building a network of fans, people who can speak on your behalf, both inside and outside of your organization, gives you credibility and reinforces your value beyond what your own golden words can do. Imagine the power of having your boss overhear testimonials from others about your skills and contributions. 360 evaluations, in which colleagues, co-workers, and even customers can be part of your performance appraisal, are another reason to let people around you know your skills and accomplishments. They may very well have an influence on your career future.

7. Internal Job Interviews

Internal job interviews are formal sessions with a distinct purpose—to secure another position in your organization. The goal is to prove the transferability of your skills and experience to the new job, demonstrate that you are ready to take on new and/or expanded responsibilities, and convince management that it is a good move for you and the organization.

Collection Section: Set Up a System

As a first act in documenting the gold nuggets of your work experience, set up an organizational system so you have an efficient way to collect and retrieve the information. Find your own comfortable method, one you're motivated to use, to make sure you have this valuable information at your lips when you need it.

If you respond best to the KISS principle—Keep It Simple Stupid—capture and store this information in computer files, file folders, or a three-ring binder.

If you're fascinated by gadgets, use your PDA or other software and computer applications to keep you entertained and dedicated to working on this task.

If decorative desk accessories, colorful pens, and artsy paper capture you, design a creative organizational system that appeals to your aesthetic sense.

As an incentive, give yourself a treat whenever you work on your organizational career system. Go to a show with friends. Shoot baskets. Take a hike. Go shopping. Have some ice cream. Soak in the jacuzzi.

Once you have a system in place, you're ready to sort through your history and write your story.

Your Story: What You've Done

Here's the heart of the chapter. The activities in this section reveal the meaty plot of your story—what sets you apart—the where, what, and how of your work efforts and accomplishments. Once you write down this impressive list of activities you will see more clearly the part you play in the organization's bigger picture, both on stage and behind the scenes.

The activities you'll draw from to write your story include:

Current Starring Role—Your Present Position
Past Performances—Your Work History
Major Roles—Key Projects You Worked On
Non-Paid Appearances—Your volunteer Activities

1. Current Starring Role: Your Present Position

An analysis of your current work includes your formal job description and all other tasks you do that aren't in the description.

A. Make a list of all your tasks and responsibilities, both those that appear in your formal job description and those that don't.

B. Review the list and then answer the following questions about the significance of your job. We've included short scripts to model how to communicate this information in career conversations.

1. How does my position support the needs of my department/organization?

"My efforts to problem-solve and update our software enable us to stay in constant communication internally as well as with vendors. Without this being operational and current, our shipping and receiving function would completely break down."

2. Whom do I have to coordinate with to get my job done?

"I have to coordinate with 13 other departments in order to get all the

information I need to organize and verify the accuracy of our latest financial products."

3. What's the most difficult part of my job?

"It's challenging to get the public's attention and support in the form of donations for our cause because it is frightening to many people. But I've developed sensitive and artful ways to entice them to pay attention and dip into their pockets."

4. What projects or tasks have yielded the most important results for my organization in the past year?

"I revised the procedures manual which improved our efficiency and reduced errors and repeated efforts."

"I saved over $20,000 by re-negotiating our maintenance contract."

"I obtained a $40,000 grant for our youth program."

"I trained our office staff on our new spreadsheet system so our efforts were completed faster, and we were more coordinated in reporting results."

2. Past Performances: Your Work History

Detailing your work history takes a little time, but it is simple to do, and the rewards are great! You'll do cartwheels when you write your next resume or prepare for your performance review, because a lion's share of the work will be done, waiting for you here in the work history. Just follow these simple steps:

A. Record the following items for each position you held prior to your current job (whether with the same company or a different one). Go back in your work history as far as you think is helpful to you in creating an inventory of your best experiences and assets.

- The organization

- Your title

- Years in the position

- The tasks and activities for which you were responsible

B. Once you've recalled the details of your work, focus on the results you achieved for your organization. In the next chapter we'll show you ways to "bottom-line" these results.

You'll be amazed at the patterns and themes you see emerge in this rich work biography. You'll also see some significant likes and dislikes. Later, in Chapter 5 we'll shine the spotlight on those "likes" to help you see your preferences more clearly and how they lead to career goals.

Here's a sample to help you get started.

Organization: The XYZ Company

Title: Training and Development Specialist

Years in the organization: 5 (1995 – 2000)

Responsibilities:
Scheduled all classes.
Evaluated and selected courses and trainers for all technical training.
Worked with HR to survey training needs.
Designed and taught the new employee orientation course.

3. Major Roles: Key Projects You Worked On

A simple listing of job tasks and responsibilities may not be sufficient to describe large and complex projects you have successfully completed or are in the process of completing. You don't want to overlook the significance of your contribution to these larger projects, so a little detail is warranted here.

With pen in hand, or fingers on your keyboard, begin summarizing projects from your Work History. Once you've got the momentum, keep going. Reward yourself at the end!

To capture your participation in major projects, record this information:

- The project name and date

- The organization

- Describe the project and your role in it

- The results you achieved

Your project description might look like this:

Project: Project Management Software Application
November 2001

Company: XYZ, Inc.

Project description:
The tours of our clients' facilities that I organized for our project managers were valuable. But they weren't realizing all the possible benefits, because there wasn't a structured way to insure follow-up. So I worked with our tech person and our software vendor to incorporate

the information gleaned at the tours into our project management software. The new application incorporated the tour information, identified action steps, and inserted pop-up reminders when it was time to get back to the client. It took about three months to complete the project because I had to get information from so many people. I had to interact with our engineers, the clients, the tech guy, and representatives from our software vendor.

Results I achieved:
The software resulted in better follow-up and follow-through and was one of the main reasons we increased our repeat business with clients. Our software vendor was impressed with the addition and is working with me to integrate this type of feedback loop into their next software package.

Once again, you'll celebrate the many skills you exhibit and the contributions you've made to your organization. And here's another bonus for all this information you're recording: Simply writing it down makes it a lot less likely that it'll slip from your memory when you're onstage in that important meeting or performance review.

4. Unpaid Appearances: Your volunteer Activities

Never volunteered? If you don't have a history of volunteer work, just accelerate to the next section of this chapter, *Fast Save*. If you do have a history of volunteerism, stop off and spend some time here. Your volunteer work may even be the heart of your story, so don't exclude it if it reveals important information about you.

Why, you may ask, are we including volunteerism in your "work" history? In many respects, volunteer work functions like paid work. It provides a structure, a goal, an end result, a process for getting the result, and the opportunity to acquire skills and knowledge.

A volunteer setting is low-risk, because volunteers rarely get fired. So often when volunteering, you'll stretch your skills and try out new ones that could be very beneficial to your organization, but ones you would never attempt to acquire in a higher-risk work setting.

Volunteer efforts also tell you a lot about the "heart part." Consider this: When you devote precious time from your busy schedule to volunteer, you are usually pursuing an interest or issue that's important to you, working on tasks you enjoy, and exercising your preferred skills. These experiences can help you bring more passion, enthusiasm, and commitment to your paid work.

In the final analysis, an employer cares more about the inventory of skills you **possess** than where they **came from**. So don't hesitate to put skills and experience derived from volunteer work "center stage." They can tell you a lot about your career preferences and help you formulate the career goals you'll present in your performance review. What's more, they can demonstrate to management important talents you have that your organization needs.

Volunteerism is Work Without the Paycheck

Because volunteer work has all the hallmarks of paid work, except for the money, treat the recording of your volunteer experiences as you did your work history. For each volunteer experience, record

- The organization

- The dates you served

- Your role

- Your responsibilities

- The results you achieved

- The application—how the skills apply to your paid work

Here's a sample:

Organization: WeServe Community Alliance

Dates: 1998 to Present

Role: Chairperson for the Antique Show Fundraiser for 3 years

Responsibilities:
Created the idea and strategic plan for an antique show fundraiser.

Promoted the idea and sold it to the board, since we'd never done it before and many people did not have experience with antique shows.

Assembled a committee, trained and motivated them.

Personally visited my contacts in the antique community and secured dealers to buy booths at our fair. Sold them on the viability of the idea.

Worked with my PR committee and developed marketing strategies to cost effectively promote the event to the public, including using the dealers' mailing list and providing dealers with marketing material to distribute at other events.

Reached out to the community and created alliances to get support and attendance.

Results I achieved:

Created and got acceptance for a new idea that had not been tried by this organization.

Persuaded dealers that they could make money (using my well thought-out strategic plan) in order to get them to buy booths and show at our antique fair.

Generated profits from adjunct activities, such as snack bar, in addition to the major revenue-generating activities of selling booths to dealers and tickets to the public.

The first year produced the most successful fundraiser in the history of the organization, and we surpassed that year's revenue in each of the two years that followed.

Application to my paid work:

My new responsibilities require me to interact with vendors and form alliances outside of the organization. This fundraiser experience demonstrates that I am successful in working with potential partners and allies to accept new ideas and support our goals.

"Fast Save"

If you don't do anything else in this chapter, use *Fast Save*! This is a speedy way to jot down important data so you can retrieve it instantly when you need it. The minutes you spend here will save you **hours** of agony later. What are the benefits? It helps you:

- Acknowledge your own efforts.

- Juice up and motivate yourself to keep going.

- Keep your positive ammunition available.

- Be prepared at a moment's notice to win.

How To Use *Fast Save*: Easy and enjoyable—that's the formula for making *Fast Save* work. Keep a *Fast Save* file folder handy at your place of work (or home), or carry a small notebook in your pocket. Use your handheld device (PDA), or tape a colored piece of paper to your desk or file cabinet. Record the task on a Post-It, stick it on your screen, and input it next time you sit at your computer. You get the idea. Use what works for you, and make it easy!

Take a few minutes daily to enter the recent tasks, accomplishments, and results you achieved in *Fast Save*. This small effort will keep your work efforts and accomplishments "top o' mind" so you never forget your value to your employer. And you have some concrete data on the tip of your tongue to offer when any opportunity for a career conversation offers itself to you. You'll be onstage with your lines ready!

Next time you need to prepare for that important performance review or career conversation you won't sweat the small stuff, because the small stuff and the big stuff are in your *Fast Save*! Simply expand those notes and watch how you shine!

When you've finished this chapter, you should have:

- A catalog—or inventory—of important tasks, responsibilities, projects, and accomplishments gleaned from your work experiences.

- A greater understanding of the contribution you make to your organization.

- The basic information you need to write the scripts for your story.

Now, in the following chapters we'll launch into the process for using these gold nugget experiences and talents to give an added star quality to your performance so you can steer your career in the direction you wish. Let's start with storytelling. Follow us, your coach, to the next chapter.

3

Docu-Dramas:
Telling True Stories That Reel in
Your Audience

A story is a powerful way to convey a message. And this book is about messages—communications about your skills, talents, accomplishments, and career vitality. So, before we coach you in a myriad of techniques for collecting and delivering this important career information, we've stopped off here in Chapter 3 to introduce the idea of storytelling. You'll find that stories, when used with the other techniques you'll learn in this book, add interest and pizzazz. They boost your ability to initiate and carry on irresistible formal and informal career conversations whenever and wherever they present themselves. "But," you say, "we're talking about 'business' here. What do 'stories' have to do with business?" Read on. We'll show you what we mean.

I coached a woman was working in the property management area of her organization and wanted to move into internal recruiting with the human resources department. She was trying to describe her skill at interviewing people to elicit important information and her resourcefulness in acting on that information. She was struggling with the words and finally in exasperation said, "Well, let me give you an example. When I was in residential real estate, I once sold a garage."

Now she had my attention. I was intrigued with how one sells a garage! She proceeded to tell her story.

The Garage Sale

I was working with a young man who wanted to buy his first house. As I questioned him about what he wanted, he seemed somewhat vague. I took him to a few homes, but none seemed to click. I noticed he kept referring to his parents' home. Finally, I said, "Could you take me to see your parents' home?" "Sure," he said. "They live real close." I asked if he needed to call first and he said no. So off we went. When we arrived, he took me right to the garage and proudly and enthusiastically gave me a tour. This garage was the most immaculate and well-organized garage I'd ever seen. Shelves and holders lined the walls and everything had its place. The linoleum floor was so clean you could eat off of it. We took a quick look at the rest of the house, but to my young client, the garage was the showpiece.

I went back to my office, got out my listings, and started calling. The owners would begin telling me about the house and I'd say, "That's ok, just tell me about the garage." I interviewed every listing until I found a garage I liked. I went out to see it and, voila, it seemed just right, so I said to the owners, "I'd like to bring my client by at 2:00 today. Do me a favor. Do not park your car in the garage. Do not even park it in the driveway; just put your car in the street." They gave me a strange look, but agreed.

At two o'clock I arrived with my client and showed him the garage. He bought the house the same day. So you see, I sold a garage. Oh yes, the house went with it.

This one story told me everything the human resources manager needed to know about this woman's flair for getting information from people and her cleverness in finding solutions. It drove home the point far more convincingly and colorfully than a recitation of her skills. I knew the manager would be impressed with her, and encouraged her to tell him that story.

The Need for Stories and Informal Career Conversations

The new fluid and fast-paced business environment requires us to think differently about careers, job security, and the job search. And a big part of that difference has to do with our increasing interdependence on each other—our colleagues, workplace friends, and business associates—people who serve as a network, a safety net, and a supportive team. They help us when the chips are down, and we, in turn, help them. With this interdependence comes the need to hone our interpersonal, communication, and networking skills.

What are the new workplace realities that create this need for interdependence and skill in forming networks and improving our communication abilities?

Job Competencies, not Descriptions. Many jobs are no longer defined by a description of tasks and responsibilities. It is becoming more common to think of a job as a fluid constellation of skills and competencies that change as the project or need changes. It's critical for job security to be able to communicate your competencies **on an ongoing basis** to your manager, management in general, your co-workers, colleagues, and others in your network.

Revolving Door Management. Changes in management are sudden and swift in today's world of mergers, acquisitions, and re-organization. New management requires you to establish your credibility all over again. You enhance your tenure with this new team if you can quickly convey your skills, accomplishments, value, and an understanding of their needs.

Obsolescence. Technology has pushed through lightning-speed changes in new knowledge, techniques, processes, and systems. A major challenge for all workers today is to avoid obsolescence by staying abreast of the new changes **and** communicating to others that your Knowledge, Skills, and Abilities (KSAs) are sharp, relevant, and up-to-date. Moreover, your network of workplace friends inside and outside of the organization provides a wealth of information and resources to help you stay current.

Collaborative Efforts. Virtual partnerships, changing project groups, and cross-functional teams are the way work commonly gets done in organizations today. You may find yourself working with a number of different colleagues and co-workers on an interim basis. As with revolving management, you need to re-establish your credibility with your new team members. Once again, if you effectively communicate to your new team what you do, how you can help, the roles you can play, the better chance you have of forging a productive and smoothly functioning team.

360 Evaluations. Another phenomenon creating a need for skills in handling impromptu conversations is the popular 360-evaluation process many organizations use today to get a "well-rounded" view of employees' performance. Artistry in finessing career conversations with peers, co-workers, colleagues, and customers is critical given the fact that they may very well become part of your evaluation team.

Network of Colleagues. A network of colleagues can be a rich source of help and information when you face a challenge at work. Asking advice from business associates who have faced a similar problem can be a quick and practical way to find solutions and sustain a high level of performance when you venture into new and difficult territory on the job. You need to maintain your credibility, so keeping them abreast of your skills, talents, projects, and results is important. Keep in touch.

"Fan Club": Referrals and Testimonials. An invaluable asset in today's job market is a "fan club" of co-workers and business associates who know your talent, can speak on your behalf, and are willing to promote you. Whether you're striving to obtain a plum project, moving elsewhere in the organization, or seeking a new position outside of your current organization, a supportive and active network will speed up the process and help insure success. Your network needs to know your talents and successes if they are to serve as your enthusiastic fan club.

Manager Updates. Once-a-year performance appraisals are insufficient for keeping your manager apprised of your progress. Use informal opportunities to communicate with your manager about your work, progress, and results. These periodic feedback sessions, even when casual and informal, will make the performance process much easier, less stressful, and more effective.

Impromptu Performances

Thus, with today's roller coaster realities, you need to be ready for impromptu performances—spontaneous opportunities to communicate your talents and accomplishments. These rich chance encounters, unlike scheduled reviews for which you can specifically prepare, require you to think on your feet and perform at a moment's notice.

The stage can be anywhere. Performances can occur any time, any place, in work and non-work related situations. They may be:

- Chance encounters with your boss in the hallway.

- Opportunities to speak up during meetings.

- Sharing and socializing with co-workers or colleagues.

- Planned or unplanned opportunities to converse with upper management.

- Meeting business associates or colleagues when socializing outside of work.

- Networking at professional, trade, or industry associations.

- Social engagements.

- Interacting with business associates outside of the organization.

- Sitting next to an interesting business person on an airplane or ski lift.

Two thoughts probably leap to your mind when you think of tooting your horn in front of peers, co-workers, friends, and new acquaintances—bores and braggadocios, not to mention that career conversations are hardly high-action adventures. But don't worry. You can captivate your listeners with engaging stories that vividly and convincingly describe your work and accomplishments. The story is a sure-fire way to make your conversations lively, effective, and comfortable to deliver. Listen closely to people who are effective, non-abrasive self-marketers, and you will catch them telling compelling stories about routine actions and results. Stories are interesting, convey valuable messages, slip easily into any conversation, and avoid that off-putting, hard-sell approach.

This Chapter as a Primer on Storytelling

In this chapter we'll focus on informal and impromptu situations where you must think on your feet. We'll show you how to develop stories to help convey your message and interject them into a myriad of conversations—formal, informal, spontaneous, and planned. This chapter is like the actor's makeup. It adds the final touch that delivers a complete and engaging package to the audience. First we'll describe the power of stories and give examples you can use in creating your own stories. Next we'll show you how to interject them gracefully into any conversation, and finally we'll describe situations that lend themselves to effective storytelling.

The Power of Stories

Stories are powerful because they contain elements that make them delightful to hear and easy to remember.

Ticklers. A story holds our attention and carries us along, step-by-step, as the "plot" unfolds. Crafting a story makes facts and information easier for you to remember and call forth at a moment's notice. A story also increases the **listener's** ability to remember the important facts and the point of the story.

> I won't forget the "garage sale" story, or this client and her talents. And I'll relish retelling the story to make the point about transferable career skills.

Vivid. A story puts flesh on the event, rounds it out, and adds detail, interest, and descriptive words. We get to see with our mind's eye the characters, the setting, the crisis or problem.

> Anyone who hears this story can picture this rare and pristinely maintained garage and most likely the inevitable comparison to one's own dirty, disorganized jungle of tools and neglected collection of junk.

Attention Grabbers. Stories have one or more elements that help captivate the listener—humor, irony, surprise, a twist, or drama, for example, that engage the emotions as well as the intellect.

> "The Garage Sale" is a unique twist on how to sell a house.

Economical. Stories can convey multiple messages in a short, condensed way. Through your natural ease and enthusiasm, you subconsciously depict personal traits, skills, and qualities that might otherwise be ignored.

> We get a vivid description of the real estate agent's skills and resourcefulness. We also gain a tacit understanding of her commitment and dedication to her clients, her willingness to go out of her way to meet their needs, and her cleverness in handling the whole situation. The story conveys a power, richness, and credibility far beyond that of a simple statement that any real estate agent might say: "I'm dedicated to my clients."

Real. Stories describe real-life events, something concrete and practical that people can easily understand and latch on to.

> We all know about garages. For most people, the need to "clean out the garage" is a constant, nagging nuisance. It's easy to see our storyteller's talent in identifying the importance of the garage and hunting down the right one. And we can understand her client's appreciation of a house with the "special" garage.

Diplomatic. Because stories are entertaining, they deliver sensitive or difficult messages in a more palatable way. You can cajole, entice, or humor your listener into accepting your message.

> Although the information in the garage story is not particularly sensitive, it allows the storyteller to convince listeners of her skills without either boring them with a dull list or overwhelming them with a heavy-handed, in-your-face delivery.

Let's look at an accomplishment of an employee who is a loan officer preparing for a performance review or career conversation, first as a straightforward statement of what took place. Let's weave the same information into a story and compare the two renditions.

> *"I created a system and checklist to proof loan applications for accuracy and completeness. Loans were taking too long to process because they had to be sent back to various departments for corrections or additional information. I created a system that included a checklist of items and a routing sheet that each person in the process had to follow. It was computerized for easy access and also available in a hard copy that could be attached to the top of the packet. We not only cut the time in half to process the papers, but also reduced the number of errors, the time it took to correct the errors, and the needless re-contacting of the customer."*

Now let's give the background, what generated her action, and tell it in story form.

Beauty and the Beast

> I took a phone call one day from one of our loan people, who's a great producer for the company. Real take-charge person. She was hot under the collar, really agitated and, to be honest, I could see why. One of her big loans was going to be torpedoed because we had made an error and it would be late. She threatened to go over our head and shake up the department. The phone almost melted in my hand.
>
> Now, it wasn't my fault, but I happened to be the unlucky party on the other end of the phone when she called, and

she was going to have my head on a platter. Since she had a few days before the deal would self-destruct, I told her I was getting on the problem and would call her back in two days. I was concerned and frustrated for her. And this was not the first time we'd had this problem. So I put my head on the problem, talked to a few people, and came up with a checklist that everyone involved in the process would use to eliminate or minimize errors and omissions. It showed me where her problem existed and how to fix it. I called her while I was putting the system together, told her I found and fixed her problem, and asked for her input into the system. She was elated and has been my fan ever since, and she's a good fan to have. We computerized the new procedure and made it easy to use. We reduced errors and cut processing time in half.

The same important information is communicated in both examples. The loan assistant came up with a checklist that reduced errors and saved time and frustration. But in the story form we get a heightened sense of the importance of the system, which makes her accomplishment seem even more significant. We gain insight into this employee's concern for customers and the people she supports. The story also demonstrates that she is good at defusing anger and solving problems.

How to Craft a Story

So what is the structure of the story that makes it so powerful and economical? Some people are natural storytellers, but storytelling can be a learned skill as well if you simply learn the basics of its structure. Depending on the story, some elements will be more important in one story than in another.

The hook. What is the appeal? Determine a hook that might be irony, humor, tension, something touching, a potential disaster, or an unusual twist? Whenever you can, tell stories that have a unique aspect. Or find what is the important or most interesting angle and build the story around it.

In "The Garage Sale," the hook is the uniqueness of selling a house by selling the garage. The storyteller teases you at the beginning with "I sold a garage once." That piques our curiosity. How on earth does one "sell" a garage?

In "Beauty and the Beast," the hook is the tension, the potential disaster if this woman takes action against the department. So the storyteller dramatizes (truthfully, but dramatically) the situation and emphasizes the woman's anger and her own reaction to it.

The plot (the action). Lead your audience through the sequence of events, making them anticipate what will happen. Hold back on the result to the end, drawing them deeper into the story.

> In "The Garage Sale," as she weaves her story she keeps us wondering and anticipating. What can she gain from seeing the parents' home? Why does he go right right to the garage? What can she do with his infatuation for a garage? The more she leads us into the story, the more we are amused and impressed at how she plots her strategy. She definitely sucks us into her story.

> In "Beauty and the Beast," the storyteller creates tension and a sense of an impending crisis as she leads us through the actions and attitudes of the angry woman, her own concerns and frustration, and the danger for the department. Will she get out of it? How will she get out of it?

As you are leading your audience through the plots of your stories, you are describing the valuable actions you took to tackle the problems, meet the challenges, and develop solutions.

Descriptive words and details. Paint a picture and emphasize important aspects of the story using colorful words and phrases.

> In "The Garage Sale," the storyteller details her thinking and her actions that led to her creative solution. We get inside her head and follow her plotting. She uses descriptive words to paint a picture of this most unusual garage so we see it clearly in our mind's eye.

> Descriptive words and phrases are very important in "Beauty and the Beast" because they help create the tension our storyteller feels as this angry woman rails at her. Note the colorful language, "take-charge person," "hot under the collar," "head on a platter," and "self-destruct."

The denouement—the end result. Denouement is a fancy literary term meaning the solution, clarification, the outcome, or the unraveling of the plot in a play or novel. This is the "they lived happily ever after" part of the story. As we've emphasized before, it's important to show the results of what you have done, so end with the happy outcome and make it fun or dramatic when you can.

> In "The Garage Sale" the client buys the garage on the spot, that very day. And by the way, the house goes with it.

In "Beauty and the Beast" our storyteller tells us she not only calms the angry woman and solves her problem, but also enlists her participation in the solution and, ultimately, enrolls the woman in her fan club.

The stories you weave into conversations can be examples of tasks, projects, and results you've accomplished on the job—in your current company and in other organizations, as the previous examples show. They can be stories from other areas of your life, as well, if they punctuate a talent, skill, or quality that applies to the current situation. Here's another example of a story that comes from a woman's personal experience, but makes a powerful statement about her ability to do the job. Leslie, who worked for a national food manufacturer, wanted a promotion into a higher level of management. The former manager of the department had been an autocrat and despot, and left with a staff feeling bruised and diminished. The decision-makers who needed to find a good leader and motivator to "heal" the department were looking outside of the organization for the next manager. Leslie created an opportunity to tell this story to the hiring team.

The Bad News Bears

I coached the Bad News Bears. When I was a teacher, I took over our intramural middle school softball team. We were scheduled to play our cross-neighborhood rival who had a reputation for being fierce competitors. We were a rag-tag group and everyone knew we didn't have a chance to win, but I was determined that we would do our best, have fun, and learn something from the experience. The coach of the other team was a tyrant. He would yell, act out, and berate the players when they made mistakes. It was sad to see the little folks hang their heads at his tirades.

I always take the opposite approach. I got my team together and told them we would do our best and have fun. I impressed upon them the importance of being a team and helping each other. When they made a mistake we talked about how to do better next time. I praised them for their attendance and commitment. We practiced drills that were fun and engaged everybody. And I made it clear that everyone would play in the game. No bench sitters on this team! We did high fives as a team before and after every practice.

Game day came. We fled onto the field, a spirited team! And you know what? We won the game. Our victory was only one point, but we won! The other team was so demoralized, they couldn't stand up against our energy and spirit. But the important thing for us was that we bonded as a team, put effort and learning ahead of winning at any cost, and had a good time. And that's how I manage people!

She got the job.

Leslie grabs us with the title, "Bad News Bears," and draws us into the action with the sad story of her rag-tag group and the nasty, mean coach. She uses colorful, descriptive words such as "berate," "tyrant," "tirades," "spirited team," and "hang their heads."

And woven through this whole story is her philosophy about people and management and her skills in leading and motivating a team. Again, this story is far more powerful than a mere recitation of her management philosophy and skills.

Here are some other story examples that come from work situations. In addition to sharing these examples to help you write your stories, we'll use them later to show you how to interject stories into career conversations and networking situations.

A Pressing Problem

A young man who worked for a manufacturing company that made tablet presses used by vitamin and pharmaceutical companies was frustrated by losing sales opportunities. He told this story as a solution to lost sales.

I had this really good customer, a great guy. We had an excellent rapport and the same philosophy about business. He was not in a position to buy a new expensive press, but was frustrated that his old press wasn't always dependable. I was frustrated too, because I didn't have a press or other products to serve him. He was looking for a new vendor, and I didn't want to lose him. I talked to a number of other people on our management team about the situation, but got nowhere.

Then I talked to a guy from back east at a trade show who said he re-conditioned machines. Bingo, I thought. So I went to our repair department that fixed broken machines and asked them if they could re-condition and upgrade machines. "We don't do that," they said. "Yes," I said, "but could you?" "Well, I guess we could." I continued discussing this with them until I felt I was on solid ground. Then I called my customer and told him we could re-condition and upgrade his machine for a third of the cost of a new machine. This was a bit risky because I hadn't told management about my scheme yet. He jumped at the chance and, what do you know, we made some good money we would have otherwise lost.

I made some money, saved a good customer, and turned the repair department into a revenue-generating entity. Oh yes, management was very happy!

Oh Rats! Save a Sinking Ship

Pat was investigating a career change from human resources into training and development. She was talking to a colleague from another company and shared this story to demonstrate her ability to design and implement an effective program.

Management was on the brink of outsourcing our entire customer service department because of constant high turnover. Our employees were fleeing like rats leaving a ship. That's because our department was not ship-shape. We weren't integrating our new people into the organization or the department! They felt isolated and disconnected from each other and from the rest of the organization. So I set a goal to develop a quality new-hire orientation and save the department.

When you really feel part of a group you want to stay. Leaving is painful. So all my efforts in the orientation program were directed at introducing them to the culture and creating a feeling of teamwork. I did not start with the traditional, dry review of policies and processes. I first set up buddy teams between new and long-time employees and encouraged them to meet in interesting places inside and outside of the company. They loved it and in some cases served as an informal mentoring relationship. I had guest speakers from other departments who were asked to tell stories about the company, the culture, and their own experience with the organization, not just deliver a lecture on their department. Of course, in our training sessions I also tucked in information about the policies and general workings of the organization that made it easy for the new hires to acclimate to the practical aspects of the company.

The heavy emphasis on culture and being a team worked! After three weeks, no one had left, whereas in the past we already would have lost two or three. In six months our turnover rate dropped by half. And we got an added benefit. The other employees who were buddies and guest speakers really enjoyed the experience. They said they got a lot out of it, felt more like a team, were pleased with their contribution, and started some informal groups and social events for their departments as well.

Tonic or the Two-by-Four

Bruce was a highly respected manager. His company wanted to send him out to poorer performing manufacturing sites to help them with productivity and improved management techniques. He needed to interview with people at the other sites in order to gain their acceptance of his efforts. He told this story when asked why he had such a high success rate with the employees he supervised.

I have a "two-drawer" employee development and performance technique that I share with employees. In my right-hand drawer I have "performance tonic"—aspirin and salve I use to work through problems with employees and help them develop, change, learn, etc. In my left-hand drawer I have a two-by-four that takes a direct and a no-nonsense approach if the employee does not respond after many efforts at coaching and support. Coaching and developing are my preferred styles, and I go out of my way to bring employees along and have good success with it. However, when I don't see progress after much effort, I give them a simple choice between shaping up or facing the two-by-four and dealing with the consequences, such as a write-up or demotion.

I had a project team, three of whom were great employees and three who were problems. They needed additional training, and the difficulties they were experiencing on the job from their lack of skills were manifested in bad attitudes and sloppy performance.

After a few attempts to help them with more training, I was still seeing a bad attitude that resulted in poor performance, tardiness, and absenteeism. So I made an appointment with each of them and indicated this was the last-ditch effort I was going to make. They all knew I was calling them on the carpet. And because my facilitative approach can be disarming, they were surprised by this turn of events. Each one hesitantly but somewhat defiantly came to my office. I explained to each that I knew we needed to get them more training. I discussed the strengths I saw in each one and the important contribution they could make. I asked for their feedback and insights, and integrating that information established performance goals.

Two of them responded immediately to the tonic. One of them resisted the tonic and persisted in demonstrating a bad attitude and poor performance. After a month, he got the two-by-four, was put on notice and let go a month later. My other two team members became two of my best people and enthusiastic fans of my two-drawer approach.

How to Interject Stories into Career Conversations

Stories are versatile creatures. They can be expanded or shortened. You can emphasize different parts of the story to make a point. And stories are appropriate in almost any situation. In this section we'll show how their flexibility allows them to be massaged for use in a variety of circumstances. Here are two ways to graciously and effectively interject a story into any conversation you are having.

1. Listen for openings in conversations

When talking to co-workers, colleagues, vendors, customers, management, or anyone who needs to know about your skills and achievements, listen for topics that allow you to tell a related story. It can be related because it's similar in content or because the situation draws on a related skill that was just introduced into the conversation. Here is an example.

Assume you're the person in "Beauty and the Beast" who designed the system to reduce errors and omissions in loan applications. You're talking to someone in another department who is influential and could be a helpful contact and resource for you in the future. You'd like this person to know your commitment and contributions to the organization. During the conversation this person says something about the importance of accuracy, angry customers, an inefficient system, or designing better systems. If any one of these topics is brought up, the door is wide open for you to say...

"I know exactly what you mean. I had an experience the other day with an error and omissions problem (or reducing process time, or developing better systems, or angry person)."

And proceed to tell your story.

"I took a phone call one day from one of our loan people..."

2. Bring up a topic that allows you to tell your story

Assume you're the person in "The Pressing Problem" story. You're at a trade association meeting where you meet a good contact who could introduce you to possible prospects. You'd like this person to know you are a trustworthy salesperson, value good customer service, and skilled in follow-through. You're both talking about what you do, and you interject into the conversation the challenges presented by the current tight market conditions. Your colleague moans about the slow activity, and the door opens for you to say...

"Yea, we've got to be alert to new ways to develop business and be sensitive to customers' bottom-line concerns."

And proceed to tell your story.

"I was working with this young fellow who was looking for a house..."

When to Use Stories Effectively

In the first part of this chapter we listed a number of career conversation opportunities. Some are highly spontaneous, such as a chance encounter with your boss in the hall, or running into a co-worker at the sporting goods store. Other situations may be planned and more formal if, for example, you call and make an appointment to talk to a colleague inside or outside of your organization, or you know you are going to make a report at a committee meeting.

Networking can be semi-structured when you deliberately attend an event where you know networking will take place, but you're not sure whom you'll meet. The preparation you've done through this book will be invaluable, and stories you've already crafted will be top 'o mind and leap from your lips. This section of the chapter will introduce sample situations and techniques you can use to massage, maneuver, and apply your storytelling skills.

1. Bring management up to date.

Assume you're the person in the "Rats" story who develops a new orientation program. You run into your boss, Chris, in the hallway. You haven't been able to talk to him for a couple of weeks and now both of you have a few minutes. You know he is concerned about the customer service turnover problem.

"Chris, glad I caught you. I hear your trip to Chicago went well."

An icebreaker is good. After a short discussion about the Chicago trip, you can simply bring up the topic. In this case, you don't need to give the character and setting because the boss will already know the background. It might be a good idea to remind him of the climax, however.

"Listen, I wanted to update you on the new orientation program we discussed a few weeks ago."

And proceed to tell your story or the part completed so far.

"I've hooked up each of our new hires with a buddy, someone who's been here a while. Plus, I've done some lively, interactive activities on the culture—the unwritten rules. It's working. The new hires are much more involved, and after three weeks no one has quit, which is unheard of. Normally, by this time we've already had two or three leave us."

2. Speak up at a meeting

Take the position of the person in the "Pressing Problem" story. Assume you've been pulled into a sales meeting in another region. They're discussing lagging sales of new machines, the saturated market, the sales quotas they can expect from the sales force, and new markets they can target.

You speak up and say,

"There's another thing we can consider as well—offering more services to our current clients."

And then follow up with:

"I had this really good customer..."

3. Demonstrate skills or experience with co-workers around the coffee machine

Let's assume you are the person in "The Garage Sale" story. You're visiting with co-workers, two of whom are in the marketing department, an area you are considering for a career move. They are discussing the cost of homes in the area, how hard it is to find what people want, a new house someone bought, etc. You chime in and say,

"I was in real estate and sold a garage once."

Obviously they'll want you to tell them the story behind the garage sale. So tell your story and point out how you had to qualify the buyer and assess his perceived needs. Then say something to the effect,

"I like this kind of sleuthing and figuring out my target audience. That's why I would enjoy marketing."

4. Market yourself or your project during formal introductions at a professional or trade association.

Imagine your name is Pat, the person in the "Rats" story. You are at an association meeting for training and development professionals. Attendees must stand up and introduce themselves. You take this opportunity to show your training experience (remember, you're considering a career in training and development) and ask for additional resources.

"Hello, I'm Pat White with XYZ company. I'm an HR specialist currently implementing a different approach to a new-hire orientation program that includes creating a buddy system and initiating them into the unwritten rules of the organization. We've already seen a drop in our turnover. I'd like to talk to anyone else who has experience in new-hire and employee orientation programs."

Notice how the story is shortened here to account for the few seconds you have available during formal introductions when an entire room of attendees must introduce themselves.

5. Communicate your talents when networking at business social events or professional and trade associations.
In this section, we demonstrate how to shorten and massage stories to fit the circumstance.

Picture yourself as the winning coach in "The Bad News Bears." Three of you are talking during the social hour at a trade association meeting. The group is discussing the challenges of managing people. You say,

"Management is a lot like parenting or coaching. I coached a softball team once that was composed of kids with little talent and experience, but I was determined they'd support each other, work as a team, learn something about baseball, and have fun. I motivated and cheered them on. The coach of the rival team had talented and more experienced kids, but he was a tyrant and just demoralized his players. We won because of our spirit and teamwork! And I use the same tactics I used with these kids when I manage my team at work."

Play the role of the salesperson in "A Pressing Problem." You are in between sessions at a trade conference, and a group of attendees from various parts of the country are talking shop around the coffee center. You are interested in following up with a couple of them as future customers or employers. The topic of conversation is the constant struggle to get and serve customers in today's market. You say,

"Well, a lot of times you've got be creative, or you've got to push the envelope and have courage to twist the arms of other parts of the organization to help you. I had a customer, a great guy who liked doing business with me, who was going to look elsewhere because he couldn't afford our new, expensive presses. I literally, with much persuasion, turned our repair shop into a revenue-generating center by having them recondition and upgrade this customer's machines so he could get better production without buying new ones. It was easy to convince him, but I had to do a fast shuffle with management and I had a real challenge in finally bringing the repair guys around. But I was determined to keep this guy as a customer and give him good service. It worked."

6. Demonstrate your skill and interest in a new area when conducting an information interview.
You, as the storyteller in "Beauty and the Beast," are interested in moving out of clerical into a position that supports the loan officers

and gives you an opportunity to deal directly with customers. You asked for an information interview with a person in the loan department who has the power to hire. You introduce yourself and share why you want to move there. You say,

"I wanted to talk to someone in a position that has a good deal of customer contact because I'm good with customers and like supporting them directly and through the officers. For example, I turned around one of our mortgage loan sales people who was very angry at a mistake our department made."

You proceed to tell your story.

Your Turn

Try your hand at writing a story. Think of something you recently accomplished. Jot down the reason you did it, the action you took, and the result. You may already have a list of these from previous work you've done in this book. Once you've selected the activity, weave it into a story using a hook, lively action, descriptive words, and the denouement (result). Here's a checklist.

Use these pointers:
Think through the:

- Hook

- Action

- Descriptive words

- Denouement (result)

Check it over. Did you:
- Find the hook or unique twist?

- Use descriptive verbs and emotion words?

- Describe your feelings and/or the feelings of others?

- Make it human?

- Make it YOU, capture your unique skill or talent?

- Heighten the energy when you could?

- Use humor?

- Describe, as interestingly as possible, your part in the story?

My Story

_____

_____

_____

_____

_____

_____

_____

_____

Be Flexible and Have Fun!

Your stories will often need to be shortened or modified to fit the context—the topic, time available, whom you're talking to, etc. Remember what we said before—all actors ad-lib. So monitor your personal style and approach the preparation for storytelling in your own special way. Some of you may want to write out every word in the story. Some of you will want to outline the stories. Some of you will simply create and replay them in your head.

If you internalize the concepts and process of storytelling and create and practice your story lines, you'll be prepared to take advantage of golden opportunities when they suddenly appear in front of you. You won't be caught off-guard. Whatever your style, weave engaging tales (true ones, of course) that showcase your sterling talents! Create away! But first, follow us, your coach, into the next chapter where we talk about the "set"—your organization.

4

The Stage Set: Your Organization

Tune in to the Set

In Chapter 1 you collected and recorded the important information about **you**. In Chapter 2 you learned how to weave these gold nuggets of information into compelling stories. Your next task, which we tackle here in Chapter 4, is to consider the setting in which you deliver this information—your organization. The more you know about your organization, the better able you will be to link your work accomplishments to its priorities—its trends, challenges, current initiatives, mission, and goals.

The organizational "set" in today's workplace, however, is more like the high seas in a storm than a stable stationary sound stage on a studio lot. The fast pace of change and the focus on global issues, mergers, and consolidations heighten the need to be informed about your organization and your role on the team if your career is to keep a steady course and stay sea-worthy. Without constant attention you may find yourself adrift on the ocean, swamped, or—worse yet—tossed overboard.

If the stage of today's market workplace is a sea of choppy, unpredictable waters, think of your career as a sailing vessel with you acting as the captain and navigator. The beauty of a sailing ship is that it works with the natural elements it encounters. Instead of fighting the sea head-on, a sailing ship tacks and maneuvers, transforming the energy of the wind and the waves into power that moves the vessel steadily along its charted course.

As you learn more about your organization you will also discover people, information, and programs available to help you steer your career. It's amazing how many employees are unaware of the resources their organization have available to them.

We'll help you chart the culture and course of your organization with thought-provoking questions and show you how to tie your work efforts to the priorities, needs, and goals of the organization.

An understanding of the company culture benefits you because it:

1. Gives you a leg up in understanding where the organization is actually sailing.

2. Helps you better understand company needs, issues, and key initiatives.

3. Identifies where your strengths and skills fit best.

4. Helps you determine the match between you and your organization.

5. Helps you communicate to management the match between you and the organization.

6. Enables you to link your efforts and accomplishments to the priorities of the organization.

7. Identifies resources the organization has available to help you manage your career.

Stage Directions: How This Chapter Will Guide You

Sea-Worthy Questions—First, you'll read a series of questions to help you identify the important information about your organization's mission, goals, and initiatives (charted course); current opportunities for it (exciting ports and safe harbors); and challenges it faces (dangerous shoals). Then you'll find some scripts that demonstrate why this information is important and how to communicate your skills so your manager sees the direct relation between your efforts and the organization's priorities.

Above and Below the Water Line—Next, we'll direct you to sources where you can discover clues about the "written" and "unwritten" rules of the organization, so you can prepare for your career conversations with these important cultural characteristics in mind.

The Bottom Line—Finally we'll provide a checklist of ways you can translate your good work into bottom-line results to give your career conversations an extra boost of power. Your work in the section below, Sea-Worthy Questions, will help enable you identify the areas your organization thinks are important to its bottom line.

Sea-Worthy Questions

To help you more easily chart the course of your organization, we've included questions and examples of some possible priorities, opportunities for it (exciting ports and safe harbors), and challenges facing it (dangerous shoals). Your department is a microcosm of these larger, organization-wide issues. As you read the list, identify the issues that are most critical to your organization and/or your department, focusing on the ones that relate most directly to the job you do. These are the ones you'll want to address in your career conversations. You may be able to add to this list. Not all items on the list will apply to every organization.

1. The Charted Course What are the organization's main goals and the current initiatives that flow from those goals? Where is the company directing its focus and resources?

- The mix of products or services provided
- Products or services management is trying to promote
- Development of new products or services
- Diversification of products or services
- Strategies to maintain a competitive edge
- Development of new business opportunities
- Implementation of new systems
- Focus on retention, learning, and employee development
- Management development/leadership
- New sales forecasts
- Acquisitions, spin-offs, downsizing
- Future goals, short term and long term

2. Exciting Ports and Safe Harbors What resources and opportunities can your organization take advantage of?

- A favorable economic/business climate
- A critical unmet need (e.g., safety and security)
- Access to talent
- The decline and/or demise of a competitor
- New legislation that will bring you customers/clients
- New trends, hot issues to which your organization can respond
- Lower costs of doing business/providing services
- Potential for new business/increase in customer base
- Potential for repeat business

3. Stormy Seas and Dangerous Shoals. What obstacles or challenges does it face? How can it protect itself and ward off potential threats?

- An economic downturn
- Unfavorable legislation/federal policies
- Current or pending litigation
- Lack of good talent
- Increasing obsolescence in products, services, or personnel
- Increasing costs
- Growing competition
- Lack of repeat business
- Changing political climate
- World events

The most important question of all for you is:

What role does my position play in helping the organization achieve its goals, take advantage of opportunities, and overcome its challenges and obstacles?

- ❑ To improve sales and revenues, business opportunities
- ❑ To maintain and expand a good image (public relations/ community service)
- ❑ To deliver quality products or service
- ❑ To provide good customer service or care
- ❑ To keep systems running smoothly for maximum reliability and productivity
- ❑ To liaison with other entities

 Scripts

These scripts demonstrate how your career conversations might sound when you tie your work efforts to the organization's priorities. We list an example of a goal, advantage, or challenge and then present a sample script that addresses that issue.

Charted Course—A goal

Acquisitions are a major priority

"Acquisitions have been the greatest influence on our growth and success in the last 5 years. My efforts to adapt and integrate the different inventory systems have made the transition in production and sales systems much smoother. We've suffered little or no downtime or additional costs because our staff, as well as the staff or of our acquired companies, have been able to use the new system effectively."

An Exciting Port—An Opportunity or Advantage

Promoting a good product mix is one of the company's strengths

"Although I work in the medical device division, I keep abreast of the products and services in other divisions as well as new products in the pipeline and those hitting the market. When I get calls from customers or vendors, it is easy for me to refer them to the right division or department and even answer some of their basic questions. It's good customer service. It saves them having to make a number of calls to get to the right person which in turn saves them time and frustration. I've even gotten thank-you notes from some of our customers."

Best-selling products and services help sell other services

"Our computer consulting side of the business is the most vigorous right now, so I always introduce it first when people ask what we do. However, I make sure I always introduce our computer and database training services because they naturally follow the initial computer training. I've been able to refer a number of potential clients to our sales and consulting staff because I've taken the initiative to introduce and promote our secondary, but growing, services."

Dangerous Shoals—A Challenge

A highly competitive industry

"The packaging business is very competitive as we all know. My efforts to work with our production and manufacturing group to design and adapt packaging that meet customers' unique specifications and packaging challenges hasve captured business from other companies. Making this part of our goals and encouraging other sales people to adopt this approach would give us a competitive edge."

Increasing cost of maintaining equipment

"Our office technology maintenance contracts were skyrocketing and having a major negative impact on our department's bottom line. We were getting pressure from upper management. And yet, our depart-ment is extremely dependent on all of our technology and vulnerable when any of it is down. Over a three-month period I investigated and evaluated over 12 possible contractors to handle our maintenance. I gathered the information, did a spreadsheet analyzing the pros and cons of each one, and compared them to each other. I asked other people in the department for feedback on their needs and preferences – what good service meant to them. In the end I selected a company that reduced our costs by 17% and gave us excellent and dependable service."

Above and Below the Water Line: Find the Organizational Information You Need

Above the Water Line

If you need to rev up your knowledge of the organization by a few knots, you can start by looking "above the water line," in all the places where organizations publish or publicize their material.

Organizations work hard on to develop their mission, vision, and goals, and they publish them. They strive to reinforce who they are and set themselves apart from the competition. They make available internal communications and other publicly accessible documents to reflect their identity, what they do, whom they serve, and how they serve them.

This information is invaluable to you because it demonstrates the organi-zation's big picture to give you an intimate knowledge of your organization so you can align your activities and career-related conversations with the organization's priorities.

Employee manual	Company history
Mission, vision, and goal statements	Sales brochures
Annual report, 10K reports	Newsletters
The Internet / company's intranet	Publicity, press releases
Advertisements	Strategic plans (if available)
Events and promotions	Sponsorships
Organizational chart	Regional business press (magazines, newspapers)

Below the Water Line

The tricky thing about the culture and "rules" is that a lot of them are not obvious. They are informal, and, like an undercurrent, hidden from view—not written down in policies, procedures, job descriptions, or memos. The culture and personality of the organization are frequently communicated by word of mouth, handed down through stories, and transmitted through repeated events, ceremonies, or activities—awards given, social events, motivational activities, gatherings, and get-togethers at the water cooler or annual picnic.

But don't think these norms are not important just because they lurk unseen beneath the surface of the organization's more obvious systems. In fact, they are often **more powerful** than the written rules because people in the organization who are alert to the "rules" and know how to use them have a decided advantage over those folks who don't.

What **can** you glean from these norms, or informal "rules," of behavior that will help you navigate your career and your conversations? You can learn:

- **Whom you can approach** for a career conversation in addition to your manager.

    Who gets easy access to people with influence?

    Who are the people that can help you?

    How to appropriately gain access to people who can help you.

    The protocol for talking to "higher ups."

- **The kind of behavior** the company rewards (hard work, long hours, minding rules, innovation, keeping the status quo, etc.), so you can emphasize those that apply to you and your job.

- **The organization's values** as expressed by actions, not just words, (people, customers, innovation, teamwork, etc.), so you can incorporate those values you agree with in your work activities and express them in your conversations.

Now let's dip beneath the surface to identify ways to help you gather information about the unwritten, informal values, personality, and style of your organization.

- **Seek out old-timers** in the organization who can remember the history of the organization and recite the "stories."

- **Identify the politically savvy people** who know the rules and are willing to share them with you.

- **Strike up conversations** with janitors, people in the mailroom, and receptionists, who can be a wealth of information.

- **Find a mentor** who can help you learn the informal rules and effectively navigate the organizational culture.

- **Find a role model** and watch how they work the political culture of the organization.

- **Watch for repeated patterns** of behavior on the part of management and employees: how they deal with each other, higher-ups, or people under them, and with problems or challenges.

- **Listen for patterns in words and metaphors.** Do you hear battle and attack-style phrases—wipe 'em off the map, plan of attack, arm yourself? Or do you hear words and phrases that connote cooperation and collaboration: teamwork, pulling together, partnering?

- **Listen for "stories,"** true or apocryphal, that capture the history and culture of the organization. What are the stories and what do they say about how things get done and people are treated?

- **What kinds of adjectives are used to describe** the way things are done: creative/innovative, accurate, thorough, efficient, economical, results-oriented? Or snide, insulting, whining, complaining, unsupportive?

- **Note how people outside** the organization (media, for example) talk about and describe your organization.

- **Is there a charismatic or dominating founder/leader** (like Bill Gates or Jack Welch) whose personality and philosophy strongly influence the culture?

Once you are clear about the rules, written or unwritten, you can work with them or around them instead of bumping into them and stubbing your toe or other important parts of your anatomy.

Gloria, a high-performing manager and marketing professional, found herself caught in a merger with a whole new management team. The new division head wanted her to do a detailed sales projection, and his rather controlling assistant wanted to make sure it got done, even to the point of telling Gloria how she should spend her time. They made these demands even though she had a good general plan and was bringing in new large, lucrative accounts. After two separate meetings to describe her efforts and success, Gloria, who was a rainmaker, realized this group was more comfortable with small droplets. The unwritten rule was "ply me with lots of data that I can read and recite, and I'll feel comfortable." Not wanting to take valuable time away from her "rainmaking," Gloria asked the assistant to help her with the report. She said, "Here are some rough numbers. Why don't you flesh out the report because you understand what's really needed?" The assistant was thrilled with the power she'd been given, the division head was euphoric about the detailed data, and Gloria was drenched in success because she kept on making rain.

The Bottom Line: Saving Time and Money

At this point you've recorded your key work experiences, skills, responsibilities, and results. You've plumbed your organization to discover its priorities as well as its personality and culture. Now you're ready to add a little spit and polish and show your bottom-line results.

Sales people have obvious markers to document their bottom-line results. If your position is a supportive function, it may seem like your immediate work activities are far removed from the dollars that flow in and out of the organization. However, if you follow the string of effects your job has on the organization through the halls and into the accounting office, you may be surprised how your efforts do impact revenue and profits. Often you are helping to reduce hidden costs and, thereby boosting profits.

To help those of you who are not in sales and other obvious revenue-generating and cost-saving areas of the organization, we've included a list of areas and ways work efforts can have a positive impact on the bottom line.

Time:

- You can save time, OR

- You can improve efficiency, so more is accomplished in the time expended

Dollars and (Common) Sense

- You can make more money—generate revenue

- You can save money—reduce costs

- You can get more for the money you spend—through higher productivity level and more efficient use of resources

Here are some examples.

1. People
(You, your co-workers, team members, or people you supervise)
You impact the bottom line when you:

- Reduce errors, improve accuracy
- Improve attitude/morale
- Increase employee attendance and retention
- Increase productivity
- Reduce staff and maintain productivity
- Increase staff and improve productivity
- Foster teamwork

2. Resources
(Supplies, telecommunications, and other technology)
You impact the bottom line when you:

- Use resources more efficiently (save time and money)
- Reduce or eliminate unneeded resources
- Obtain needed resources to maintain/improve productivity
- Reduce equipment breakdown
- Reduce cost of acquisition
- Reduce maintenance costs

3. Information
(Numbers, databases, ideas, information, facts, specifications)
You impact the bottom line when you:

- Obtain essential information/data
- Reduce amount needed
- Streamline the flow
- Improve flow to the people who need to get it
- Identify the most important information/data
- Improve the accuracy of the information/data
- Reduce errors in information/data
- Improve the ease and speed in accessing information/data

4. Process

(A series of activities dealing with the interaction and flow of people, resources, and information)

You impact the bottom line when you:

- Add important steps
- Eliminate unnecessary or redundant steps
- Change or alter the sequence of the flow
- Improve the parts of the process (people, information, resources)
- Add people involved in the process
- Eliminate people involved in the process
- Communicate the importance of the process
- Improve skills in using the process

5. Customers

The way you handle customers can add dollars to the bottom line or cost you money. Since customers and clients are the lifeblood of every organization, we've put them into a separate category to discuss. You don't have to be the sales person to influence many of these factors that lead to good customer relations and sales!

You impact the bottom line by:

- Creating more satisfied customers
- Delivering good products
- Delivering good service
- Improving service
- Improving products
- Solving customers' problems
- Staying in touch
- Following up and following through
- Salvaging customers who were taking business elsewhere
- Getting repeat customer sales
- Adding new customers
- Enhancing sales to current customers

Before we have you start using these ideas to document your bottom-line results, let's look at some examples., gathered together in a chart.

CHART TO ANALYZE YOUR BOTTOM-LINE RESULTS
(Examples that are taken from different people)

Area	What you did	How you influenced
People	Helped a co-worker improve the skill on a task he does 20 times a year.	Saved at least 2 hours time in the completion of the task.
People	Talked to my employee about career development. Acknowledged the need to look to increase responsibility level. Need more challenge. Discussed tardiness.	Employee came in on time 5 days a week instead of the usual 2 days a week. Saved 3 days of tardiness.
People Customers	Reduced one person on project #1 and moved him to project # 2, which was badly understaffed.	Project #1 still came in on time. Project #2 came in 2 months earlier than expected because of additional staff person and generated 2 more months of revenue than had been anticipated. Client was happy and gave us their next contract.
Resources	Re-negotiated maintenance service contract for computers and office equipment.	Reduced monthly fee.
Resources	Discovered 200 outdated computers in a storage unit	Sold computers to a re-seller and terminated rental on the storage unit to save money
Information	Revised a form to gather information more clearly and logically	Reduced errors and time to hunt down accurate and correct information. Support staff saved approx. 12 hours a week in combined time saved from increased accuracy.
Process Customers	Reduced the time it took to get materials from the warehouse to the assembly plant and then to the customer	Saved approximately 5 days time to deliver goods to customer

Your Turn

Now that you've seen some examples, go back to your Current Job and Work History activities. Make a list of those tasks and accomplishments that you can quantify, and, using our guidelines (and any you design), show your organization how you've contributed to the bottom line!

Area	What you did	How you influenced

The Next Phase

Your story is really taking shape. But there's one more critical element before you can be completely ready to step onstage for your performance review. What are you going to tell your manager about your career goals? We've looked at the wonderful things you **do**, but what is it you **like**? To find career satisfaction and to be a truly productive worker for your organization you need to base your career goals on your preference. What are your preferences in tasks, roles, and responsibilities? What skills do you love to use? In what way do you want to have an impact? Follow us, your coach, into the next chapter where we'll tackle this important and exciting part of your performance review preparation process.

5

The Character:
Your Career Preferences
and Goals

To play a role convincingly, actors must "get under the skin" of their characters to uncover what drives and motivates them. This chapter on self-discovery—identifying your career preferences and goals— helps you clarify what drives and motivates you and makes work satisfying and rewarding. What does self-discovery have to do with your performance review—or any career conversation for that matter? Everything!

The performance review is a stage specifically designed for you to communicate your value to the organization and where you want to go with your career, whether it's staying where you are or moving elsewhere in the organization. Your ability to express your career needs and goals thoughtfully and realistically **and** to enlist your manager's support in attaining these goals is, perhaps, the most important part of the performance review and your self-managed career process.

Making good career choices is a matter of fit between your talents, skills, and preferences and the job opportunities your organization presents along the way. It's like actors looking for the roles that will best showcase their talents. Your task, when you take a proactive approach to your career and your performance review, is to help management see your best fit.

And making a fit starts, first, with you knowing your key strengths and what you want. Only when you are clear and confident about your direction, can you convincingly state your goals and get management to support you in achieving them. Imagine you're seated in a restaurant. When the waiter asks what you'd like, your only response is, "*Something good.*" The waiter can't help you if you can't be more specific about what you want.

How This Chapter Will Coach You

You can start the "matching" process right here in this self-discovery chapter. Easy-to-use descriptions and checklists help you discover revealing patterns of work motivations and preferences and give you the words to communicate them in your career-related conversations. Once you recognize these startling patterns and answer the questions *Who am I?*, *What do I want?*, *Where do I fit?*,

51

and *How can I best serve my organization?*, you will have more information to set realistic career goals. And when you enter the stage for your performance review, you won't be at a loss for the right words or stumble over your lines.

First we introduce Seven Self-Discovery Pieces that help you uncover factors critical to your career satisfaction. If you need, or would like, more in-depth assessment than is offered in this brief presentation, check for classes offered by your organization or the extended education programs and career centers of your local colleges and universities. You can also read one of the many books available on the topic, search the Internet for career assessment sites, or hire a career counselor to coach you through an assessment process.

In the second part of the chapter we coach you to set career goals. To help you, we present six different ways you can move in your organization, as given in Beverly Kaye's book, *Up is Not the Only Way*. We also address what to do if you finish this work and still don't know where you want to go. Plus we handle that tricky topic, how to move out of your organization, if you feel that's the only choice for you.

Seven Self-Discovery Pieces

When you're in the process of making an important life decision you usually run through a list of criteria—things you want and need. For example, an actor choosing a role will consider salary, the director and other actors, the strength of the script, the reputation of the theater company or production studio, how badly he needs to work, the time involved, location, and how it will potentially affect his career. Whether it's in your head or captured on paper, a list of criteria guides your decision-making, steering you toward things you want and away from things you don't want, to help you make the best choice possible given the information you have at the time.

Career decisions are among the most important decisions you make in a lifetime, so we've provided you with Seven Self-Discovery Pieces that serve as a "career criteria checklist." The Seven Self-Discovery Pieces help you assess your career satisfaction factors, set career goals, and evaluate career opportunities when they present themselves. When you can describe what each piece means to your work life, you will have a template you can lay over any career opportunity, now and in the future, to see if the opportunity matches what you want and need.

The Seven Self-Discovery Pieces also give you words and phrases to help you convey your talents, accomplishments, skills, career preferences, and goals. We'll lace the chapter with sample scripts to demonstrate how you can deliver this information effectively during career conversations.

Hint: As you read and answer the questions posed in each of the seven pieces, you may want to refer to the work history and other items you completed in Chapter 2, Preparing Your Story. You will find some of the answers, or clues to the answers, waiting for you there.

1. Working with People, Data, or Things

All work efforts depend on a combination of people, data, and things. It's where you want most of your energy to be concentrated that counts. We'll break these apart so you can examine each one.

- **Working with People:**
  When asked what they want from a job, many people say, "I want to work with people." The joy, satisfaction, and reward you derive from working with people will depend on **whom** you work with, **how** you work with them, and **how much time** you want to spend with them.

  Ask yourself:
  - ❑ What kind of people do I want to work with?

  - ❑ How (in what way) do I want to help, serve, or collaborate with them?

  - ❑ How much time do I want to spend with them during a workday?

- **Working with Data**
  Many people don't recognize how much they enjoy working with information, ideas, concepts, and numbers. Again, the reward you get from working with data will depend on **what kind** of data or information you like to deal with and **how** you prefer to work with it.

  Ask yourself:
  - ❑ What kind of information do I want to handle (facts, theories, concepts, people-related, scientific or technical, etc.)?

  - ❑ What do I want to do with data (find, organize, create, analyze, present it)?

  - ❑ How much of my day do I want devoted to handling information?

- **Working with Things**
  To be happy at work, do you need to interact with things—tangible items you can touch, fix, re-arrange, or build? Many jobs today involve primarily knowledge and people-oriented work. But some folks derive the greatest satisfaction from using their hands and working with things.

Ask yourself:

❑ Do I need to work with things in order to be happy in my job or career?

❑ What kind of things do I want to work with (tools, equipment, machines, decorative items, etc.)?

❑ What do I want to do with things (fix, arrange, make, present them)?

2. Roles You Play With People

Feeling comfortable and enjoying the **way** you work with people improves your general job satisfaction. Sometimes you can't work well or happily with perfectly nice people because you're uncomfortable with or dislike the way you have to work with them.

Ask yourself: What role(s) do I prefer to play with people?

❑ Counselor

❑ Resourcer

❑ Entertainer

❑ Manager

❑ Leader

❑ Expert/consultant

❑ Liaison

❑ Mediator

❑ Negotiator

❑ Educator

❑ Marketer

❑ Advocate

3. Skills – Technical, Personal, Transferable

People who love their work are using their best and most preferred skills. It's hard to compete with others who are happy in their work if you don't love yours, because they will have more energy and spirit for what they do. They're jazzed and juiced, creative and committed. Of all the pieces in the career satisfaction puzzle, this is usually one of the most important.

There are three types of skills. **Technical** skills are job-specific skills such as computer skills. **Personal** skills are the qualities that reveal what you are like. For example, tenacious, dependable. **Transferable** skills tell what you "do" and are described by verbs; they are portable skills that you take with you wherever you go—home, work, play, and from one career to another. We've included a short list of technical, personal, and transferable skills to give you a jump-start in identifying these important abilities and qualities.

- Technical Skills
  - ❏ Accounting
  - ❏ Research
  - ❏ Typing
  - ❏ Science
  - ❏ Artistic
  - ❏ Computer
  - ❏ Laboratory work
  - ❏ Medical
  - ❏ Mechanical
  - ❏ Drafting

- Personal Skills
  - ❏ Tenacious
  - ❏ Humorous
  - ❏ Forward thinking
  - ❏ Calm
  - ❏ Reliable
  - ❏ Action-oriented
  - ❏ Poised
  - ❏ Charming
  - ❏ Fair
  - ❏ Hardworking
  - ❏ Team-oriented
  - ❏ Innovative
  - ❏ Energetic
  - ❏ Punctual
  - ❏ Optimistic
  - ❏ Decisive
  - ❏ Charismatic
  - ❏ Flexible

- Transferable Skills
  - ❏ Gather information
  - ❏ Communicate in person
  - ❏ Write
  - ❏ Lead
  - ❏ Speak publicly
  - ❏ Manage
  - ❏ Teach/train
  - ❏ Problem solve
  - ❏ Analyze
  - ❏ Evaluate
  - ❏ Create
  - ❏ Listen
  - ❏ Read people
  - ❏ Market
  - ❏ Sell
  - ❏ Promote
  - ❏ Organize
  - ❏ Implement
  - ❏ Defuse conflict
  - ❏ Negotiate
  - ❏ Plan
  - ❏ Develop policies
  - ❏ Advise/consult
  - ❏ Delegate

Ask yourself:
- Which skills and qualities do I possess?
- Which ones do I most enjoy using/exhibiting?
- Which ones would I like to acquire or develop?

Add any other skills and qualities you think of:

_____

_____

4. Work Environment

Environment is a broad term that encompasses everything from location and premises to the psychological atmosphere and culture of the organization.

Ask yourself: How do I fit with the organization's
- Culture (tone and atmosphere)
- Premises and space arrangement
- Size
- Pace and flow of work
- Degree of structure and formality of job descriptions and reporting lines
- Mission and goals

5. Attitude Toward Work

What does "work" mean to you? Lance Morrow in a Time magazine editorial said, "Work is the way we tend the world, the way we connect." Work, to Lance Morrow, means more than a paycheck. To him, work has meaning for society as well as for the individual. Attitude toward work is not just a matter of whether you like work or not, it's the role work plays in your life and the value you place on work. Is work just a "place-holder," something you must do? Or does it influence your esteem and self-concept? If so, how?

Ask yourself: Is work a way for me to
- ❑ Get a paycheck
- ❑ Express myself
- ❑ Be creative
- ❑ Have influence
- ❑ Help others
- ❑ Make a difference
- ❑ Stimulate my brain

- ❑ Apply skills and knowledge
- ❑ Help society
- ❑ Take up hours between morning and night

6. Essentials You Must Have

Essentials are just that, the "must have's," because they put food on the table and clothes on your back. The funny thing about Essentials is that they're very important, but, unlike some of the other more abstract Self-Discovery Pieces, not very hard to figure out.

Ask yourself: what do I need in terms of

- Financial rewards
- Benefits
- Training
- Vacation
- Personal time

7. The Heart Part

Work is best when it is simply another manifestation of your authentic self, when it is an instrument for letting you act on the world in a way you feel is significant and uses your best and most preferred talents. This is when work taps the "heart part," or, to use a word career counselors are fond of, passion. Passion for your work can flow from three different sources. Work may allow you to:

Apply a certain skill or flair that brings you great satisfaction—for example, training, managing, or troubleshooting (as long as they are done in the right situation).

Follow a strong interest—for example, computers, sports, travel, building, or design.

Play out an issue, something that you care about very much and feel is an important way to impact the world—help children, the elderly, support a political philosophy, foster fitness and good health, or teach people to be resourceful.

Ask yourself:

- Am I an issue-oriented person?
- If so, what are my passions, issues, or interests? What do I really care about?
- Do I need to play my issue(s) out in my work, or can they stay avocational?

Putting yourself through self-discovery every time you face an important career choice, whether it be a new position, a possible project to undertake, or a committee to join, will help you make the right decisions and keep your career vital and rewarding.

> A fellow who had gone through a thorough self-discovery process called his career counselor to tell her of his latest move to a new position. He had made a major career change after his work with the counselor, moved to another company in the same industry three years after that, and now had moved on to a second position in the current company. "Well," said the career counselor after hearty congratulations were given, "did you use the career process you learned?" "Oh, yes, I always do. The self-discovery exercises were so powerful. They keep me honest about what I really want to do and what I do well. I'm not seduced by opportunities that appear to offer goodies, but are really not right for me."

What Did You Uncover in This Self-Discovery Exercise?

What did you unearth through this brief self-discovery exercise? Did you see patterns of likes and dislikes? Did you identify the skills you most like to use? Did you find roles that allow you to work with people in the way you prefer? Could you determine how well matched you are to your environment?

Did you discover concepts, words, and phrases to describe factors that are critical to your career satisfaction and productivity? These Self-Discovery Pieces give you a vocabulary to use when you talk to your manager so you can avoid vague expressions such as, "I want to work with people" or "I need to be more creative."

Do you need more work on self-assessment to answer these self-discovery questions?

Read the following scripts to see how to weave these self-discovery lines into your career conversations. Notice how the people in these examples connect their preferences to career goals.

Scripts

Working with people
"One of the reasons I'm happy and successful at my job is because I get to interact with a lot of people from different departments, which is helpful to the organization, because I have the ability to get along with a wide variety of personalities."

Working with data

"I could be more productive if Chris, who has great people skills, could take help-desk time and let me have more quality time to review and organize the data and information we are lacking right now. The lack of information makes our help-desk people less effective with customers than they might be. If I spent a little more time getting the information to them, I believe it would improve our customer service."

Roles with people

"I'd like to explore the possibility of training people in other departments who are having the same problems I fixed here. I like the 'educator/trainer' role and get good feedback on my talents in this area."

"I've enjoyed working as a team leader because I've been able to counsel and direct people to the tasks they like and perform competently."

Skills

"I've discovered I'm very good at defusing conflict. I'd like to add some labor relations experience to my compensation and benefits portfolio of skills."

"I like the analysis and problem solving that are part of the quality assurance work that I've done. I'd like to consider doing work as a business systems analyst because of the process nature of the work and the type of analysis and problem solving I would get to do."

"Training and educating have been a large part of the work I've done in sales with our customers, and I've been very effective at it. I'd like to do sales training for our staff and make them better at informing and training customers on our products and follow-up services."

"I'm good at strategic planning, particularly when I can create order out of chaos. I like to take disorganized systems and make them work better, or orchestrate the start-up of a new department or division where I have to create and design the whole thing!"

Environment

"We have a very fast-paced environment in this PR and production department. I'd like you to consider me for a position in research that would allow me to use my information-gathering skills and have more solitary work time. I've done research in other positions I've held here, so I'm confident I could do the job."

"I like it here and feel I excel in part because of the creatively charged, fast-paced environment."

Essentials

"I would like some advanced training in negotiating and labor relations since more of my time is being consumed with these functions, and they are critical to the organization."

"Approximately 40 percent of my time is spent on research and the development of complex proposals. I would like to work two mornings at home where I have fewer interruptions and could complete the lion's share of this proposal writing. It would be more productive for the organization because my full attention in the office could then be devoted to my other tasks. The compartmentalization of these tasks is more efficient for the department."

The heart part

Apply a skill:

"I thrive on trouble-shooting and have done it very effectively for our company when given a chance. I would like to work with our field offices that are in trouble or less productive. I believe I can turn them around."

Follow a strong interest:

"I've taken courses and done extensive self-study on our major software programs and am fascinated with the business systems applications. I'd like to get more involved in our IT department, possibly moving into project management."

Play out an issue:

"I feel very strongly about the importance of communication and dialogue and have improved the morale and productivity of our department by creating better communication systems. I would like to serve on our new company-wide committee to review our mission and goals and how we communicate them throughout the organization."

Now that you've stopped to examine your career preferences and your work likes and dislikes, you're ready to think about your future with the organization—where you'd like to go with the organization and how they will benefit from helping you get there.

Setting Your Career Goals

Sometimes you'll feel a real tension between what the company sees for you in their organization and what you want for yourself. There's no "right or wrong" here! Both you and your company benefit when this tension is eliminated, and that starts with **you!**

Let's assume the core of your goal is career satisfaction. You must identify and take charge of your career wants, preferences, and goals. You're the only one who truly knows what's in your heart. This is the time to be **honest** with yourself, about **yourself.** The company can't do it for you. No one can do it for you. Here's why this works: When you're honest with yourself and clear about what you want and there's a fit with your company, it's a win-win for you **and** your company. When there's a mismatch, it's a lose-lose for both.

Remember: This is a no-fault/no-blame deal. Both you **and** your company are seeking the same thing—a win-win, satisfying situation for both of you.

The combination will pay off big time. And the biggest reward, for you and your company, is achieving the goal you set. So, here's where you'll get ready and actually set those all-important goals to "plot" your career. And when you've done that, you'll have determined:

- What you really want.

- The game plan to get it.

- What you must do to get it.

- How management can help you get it.

The same requirements apply whether you stay in your current role, look for something else in the organization, or look outside the organization if there's no room at the inn.

There's no rush. Take your time. This is very important work. Just as in play writing, you may need to run alternate goals (plots) up the flag pole to find one you're excited about pursuing and willing to work hard at to achieve. Once you've done that, the rest falls into place.

"But," you ask, "what happens if my career goal is something the organization can't or won't provide or says it must delay?" **Plenty.** You still have much to gain from taking control of your career goals and approaching your organization with a plan. In that effort alone you illustrate your value to the organization. You demonstrate that you:

- Take initiative and are proactive about your work.

- Value your career.

- Stay attuned to the organization's goals.

- Are eager to find the best fit to help the organization meet its goals.

- Are resourceful in generating ideas about what YOU can do to further your career.

You have everything to gain because:

- Your initiative and resourcefulness will make it easier to enlist the support of management.

- You will be noticed as an employee who has the interest of the organization at heart.

- You'll stay on the radar screen as someone targeted to develop and promote, if that's what you want.

- Management will now know HOW to help you and be better able to provide you with valuable ideas, information, and resources to help you achieve your goals or set new ones, now or in the future.

- You'll be clear about who you are and what you want, how determined you are to get it, and what you have to do to achieve it.

Six Major Options

You have six major options as you consider **if** and **where** you want to move. But before we introduce them, take this quick inventory to help pinpoint your career issues and see what options might be best for you.

A Quick Career Decision Inventory
Check as many items as apply.

___ 1. I like the work I currently do

___ 2. I don't see a reason to make a change

___ 3. I feel sufficiently challenged and stimulated by my current job

___ 4. My current job gives me what I want from work

___ 5. I need new challenges

___ 6. I would like to acquire new skills

___ 7. I would like to acquire new knowledge

___ 8. I need more training and development

___ 9. I want to advance in my career

___ 10. I want more money

___ 11. I need higher-level responsibilities

___ 12. I want work that holds more interest, passion for me

___ 13. I want a better fit for my skills and talents

___ 14. I want out of my current situation

___ 15. I'm too stressed with my current level of responsibility

___ 16. I feel burned out

___ 17. I want to do a good job but have less pressure

___ 18. I'm not sure my personality fits into this culture

___ 19. I don't have a strong interest in the organization's products/services

___ 20. I don't see a place in the organization for my skills, talents, and/or interests

Let's see what your answers reveal about which of the **six career decision choices** might be right for you. These are the choices, discussed in detail below:

1. **Stay Where You Are**
2. **Enrich the Job You Have**
3. **Move Up**
4. **Move Laterally**
5. **The Stress-Saver Move Down**
6. **Move Out**

OPTION 1 - Stay Where You Are

If you marked questions 1-4, you're happy where you are! But job markets, like audiences, are fickle—ever-changing and unpredictable. Even though you remain where you are, you'll be wise if you follow the advice of Jack Welch, former CEO of General Electric: "Be eager to stay, but ready to leave."

Stay sharp. Be dedicated to doing your best for your organization. Achieve results and communicate them to the organization whenever you can. Career conversations with management and your performance reviews are important opportunities to drive home your value to the organization.

OPTION 2 - Enrich the Job You Have

If most of your checkmarks fall in items 5-8, you may be a candidate for job enrichment. Finding job satisfaction and growth does not necessarily mean you have to move to another position. Career enrichment means staying where you are and **enhancing** your current position to expand the scope, visibility, autonomy, challenge, attractiveness, meaningfulness, or potential of the job. Often you enrich the job you have to give yourself additional skills and experience to move on to another position at a later date.

Enriching your job means making a qualitative difference in the work you do. It's NOT just taking on "more tasks." Here's a list of ways you can enrich your job. Your efforts in the previous chapters will give you clues to the kind of enrichment activities you can undertake given the needs and preferences you've identified.

- Improve your current performance by identifying an area of weakness and deliberately working to improve that area.

- Take on a new skill-building task, project, or event you find enjoyable.

- Look to build "hot skills," those skills currently in demand.

- Take on a task or project that allows you to acquire new knowledge and information, particularly new, cutting-edge knowledge important to the organization.

- Find a task, project, or event that puts you in touch with others in the organization so you expand your network and gain greater recognition and increased credibility within the organization.

- Ask to take total responsibility for a task or project for which you now assume only partial responsibility.

To stay where you are and "grow in place is an intelligent choice," says Beverly Kaye, author of *Up is Not the Only Way*. Enriching your job infuses your work with new life and vitality. Are you a candidate for job enrichment? What ideas and suggestions could you suggest to your boss in your next career conversation or performance review?

OPTION 3 - Move Up

If you find checkmarks in numbers 9-11, your decision may require a promotion so you can achieve a higher level and/or broader scope of responsibilities and the increase in compensation that goes with them. Promotion often involves the management of people. Consider your interest, skills, and readiness to take on a management position. If you are already managing, evaluate the degree to which you want to continue functioning in a management capacity.

OPTION 4 - Move Laterally

Marking items 12-14 indicate that you may need a change in the work that you do and the functions you perform. Rather than staying in place or rising higher in your current area, you may need a lateral move to another part of the organization where your interests and desire to use new skills can be satisfied. For example, you may want to move from human resources to training or development, or from IT (information technology) to operations.

OPTION 5 - The Stress-Saver Move Down

Checkmarks 15-17 indicate you are under too much stress. If the pressure you feel is a result of the **responsibility** that comes with the **level** of position you hold, you may want to consider a move down. Although it can pose some risk to your future with the organization, it may be the only reasonable option if it saves your sanity. This decision requires careful preparation and presentation to your family or significant others, as well as to the organization. But if you handle it in a reasonable manner and continue to demonstrate your value to the organization, both you and the organization will gain in the end.

OPTION 6 - Move Out

In any discussion about career choice, we can't ignore the option of leaving your organization. You may not be doing handsprings at the thought of launching a job search, and your company will not want to lose a valuable employee. But if you have strong career needs and goals and the organization cannot find a fit for you, both you and your organization need the courage to "let go." In the long run it will be in their best interest as well as yours. Remember, we're after a win-win here. But before you make a drastic decision to move out, make sure you give careful, thorough consideration to Options 1-5.

What If I Don't Know What I Want?

Start with Self-Discovery

Not sure which way you want to move? Do you still need to find a stage in the organization where you can play your favorite role? Then **explore**, and **start** with what you've already learned about yourself in Chapters 2 and 4. Ask yourself these questions:

1. What key experiences have I had with this organization?

2. Which of these have showcased my best skills and abilities?

3. Which of these have I most enjoyed using?

4. What other skills and abilities would I like to use and apply?

5. Where's my "pay-off"? In other words, what important contribution can I make to the organization that will give me personal satisfaction as well?

6. Where in the organization do I see the opportunities to use these abilities, make these contributions, and find satisfying work?

Investigate Opportunities to Find the Right Role in Your Organization

Use these techniques to scout out roles (positions) you can fill in your organization that meet the criteria you've listed above.

1. **Company Savvy.** Search your company for opportunities. Since you've done this in Chapter 4, revisit those suggestions and apply the ones that work for you. Read the company literature and review the company organizational chart or other materials that detail the different divisions and departments of the organization. Do you have transferable skills that can allow you to move elsewhere in the company?

2. **BossTalk©.** Share with your manager what you already know about yourself, and ask for input and feedback about positions that may match your skills, experiences, and needs as you've expressed them. Later, we'll give more details about how to do this effectively.

3. **HR.** Call someone in Human Resources and discuss the possibilities he or she sees for you given your skills and needs.

4. **Job Posting.** Scan the organization's formal or informal systems for posting or communicating available jobs.

5. **The Grapevine.** Keep your eyes and ears open. Weed through the gossip and tune into happenings in the organization that may lead to new job opportunities.

6. **Joiner.** Offer to serve on a company-wide committee. Go to company gatherings and social events (even if you're not an extrovert). Hang around the water cooler. Tune into information about happenings in other areas of the company. A job may be lurking there.

7. **Network, Network.** And then network some more. Although you're doing this when you hang around the water cooler, tune into the positive grapevine, and join committees, look for other formal and informal opportunities to network, such as professional associations and community activities.

Talk to People

The best information about a career or position is in the hearts and minds of the people doing the job! So why not go to the source? Talk to them! You can hold these "informational interviews" with people inside and outside of your organization. Both can be invaluable to you as you seek to arrive at a decision and make yourself marketable.

Once you've identified the folks you want to talk to, **prepare**, so you don't waste their time or yours. And don't take these conversations lightly. It's easy to ask a few questions, get to know the person, have a good time, and walk away with no clear vision of the job. When you finish an informational interview, you want to feel that you've slipped into their costumes and played their role. To do this, you need to have done prior research on the position and prepared a list of probing questions, such as the ones here, to uncover the real roles people play in a career:

- What does your job description say you do?

- What do you "really" do?

- What do you like best about your job?

- What do you like least about your job?

- What would most people in the field say are advantages to this career?

- What would most people in the field say are disadvantages of this career?

- What is the easiest/most difficult part of your job?

- What key skills does this job take?

- What knowledge and expertise are required?

- How did you get into this field?

- What would it take for someone with my background to get into this field?

- Can you suggest other people I can speak with or resources I could access to gain a better understanding of this position/career?

A Word About Moving Out

If Options 1-5 don't resonate with you, you may need to move on to another organization, but **make a gracious exit**. It's hard to leave when the organization feels like family, so it's usually easier to make a gracious exit under these circumstances. However, if your relationship with the organization has soured, it's often easy to leave and hard to make a gracious exit. Remember that old adage about burning bridges. DON'T! You can get scorched.

It's in your best interest to leave on a positive note. Think about it. Aside from the immediate release of pent-up anger, what do you have to gain from a bitter and confrontational departure? A quick and fleeting "feel good" is satisfying for a moment, but can jeopardize your future. Your reputation, like a shadow, follows you everywhere and can spring on you when you least expect it. Make a gracious exit, no matter what, and your reputation won't cast a dark shadow over your future prospects.

Burning bridges can derail an otherwise successful career journey. Here are some reasons why you want to leave with your bridges intact:

- You may need a reference from them, now or down the road.

- Someone in the organization has information/resources you need.

- The object of your "acting out" shows up as a manager or co-worker in another organization where you work.

- You keep meeting them at professional or industry groups.

- They suddenly appear in a position with the power to recommend you, or NOT, for a job or project.

- They show up as a customer or vendor with whom you must interact.

Does this mean you can't have an honest discussion about your issues? NO. You can. Just be diplomatic, constructive, and strategic. Think through the ramifications and your long-term goals.

Kudos

Now that you've completed this watershed chapter and taken charge of your career future, dive into Chapter 6, where, as we've promised, you'll find tips and scripts from your coach to help you implement these all-important goals!

6

Dress Rehearsal for the Performance Review

Lots of sweat and preparation go into a production before an actor appears onstage opening night. **Congratulations!** You've put in the sweat and preparation in the last five chapters. Now you're just about ready to perform.

Performance Appraisals in a Perfect and Not-So-Perfect World

In a perfect world your manager would be a master at giving feedback and have only your best interest at heart. Performance reviews would follow an ideal format and be conducted smoothly and on time. You would have two weeks with nothing to do but prepare for your review.

On a more serious note, there are some things you should expect a performance review to do:

- Be an objective, fair, honest, and tactful evaluation of your performance.

- Help you improve.

- Set clear expectations and goals so you know how to proceed in doing your job.

- Be supportive and motivating, even when the review is more critical than you would like.

- Deal with sensitive issues, sensitively.

- Adhere to organizational policies and legal procedures.

However, there's no perfect world. The truth is, performance reviews are often imperfect, and there are good reasons why.

Employee evaluations make everyone nervous because **everyone**, including the boss, is "onstage" and, to some extent, laid bare before the bright lights. As Amy Joyce says in her *Washington Post* article (Sunday, March 24, 2002), "Why Wait to Evaluate," "They [performance reviews] make the worker bees feel as if they're walking into the principal's office. And the managers find them even worse." Managers, unless they are downright ogres who love confrontation, shrink from giving bad news and critical advice. Many managers feel uncomfortable giving **any feedback** at all, positive or negative.

Performance reviews can be stressful, even when they are positive. The discomfort felt by parties on both sides of the desk often causes organizations and employees to handle the performance process badly, or avoid it altogether. Whether the system works well or not, you need to be prepared and ready to take control of your evaluation. Your career can suffer if you don't.

Understanding Your Manager's View of the Performance Appraisal

As you face your performance review, take a look at the process from the other side of the desk. Your manager may face challenges and constraints with the appraisal process that have nothing to do with you. Understanding your manager's perspective can inspire and guide you to be resourceful and self-reliant in preparing for your performance evaluation so you can help your manager help you! What concerns and obstacles might managers face? They may:

- Believe the performance appraisal process an exercise in busywork.

- Find the organization's appraisal system poor, inadequate, or difficult to use.

- Feel pressure that they, too, are highly accountable and being evaluated on their mandate to conduct accurate and timely employee reviews.

- Lack confidence, skills, or training to do an adequate job of evaluating and communicating with employees.

- Feel they do not have the support of the organization.

- Fear grievances and litigation.

In each case you have everything to gain and nothing to lose by being proactive in the appraisal process and meeting your manager more than halfway. You can minimize each one of these obstacles if you prepare, as we will show you in this book, to communicate and demonstrate your skills, knowledge, positive attitude, work activities, and results.

Your clear, specific, and result-oriented statements about your accomplishments and how they link to the organization's goals will dispense with any sentiment that **your** appraisal is mere busywork. The preparation you do can overcome limitations in the design and/or execution of the performance appraisal system by filling gaps and expanding important information about your achievements. Furthermore, your sterling performance in the review process can compensate for your manager's fears or lack of skills because you are doing much of the legwork and carrying the water, so to speak. What's more, you'll demonstrate that you appreciate your manager's feedback and take the performance review seriously even if the organization does not. And last but not least, you'll make your manager look good!

Your Off-Stage Coach: Handling the Dress Rehearsal

This chapter takes you to, and walks you through, the dress rehearsal. It's where you bring together all the work you've done in the previous chapters so you can create a "script" and be ready to walk on any stage and give a winning performance, star that you are! This is where the director sits back and listens, because you're prepared and rehearsed and are ready to perform your part for an audience—your manager.

First, we put the performance review in its place. We discuss why it's an important "main event," but not the only one in your career journey.

Second, we have a "rev-up" section with tips to help you get started and make the whole process flow smoothly.

Third, we describe different performance appraisal elements and how to compensate for weaknesses and take advantage of the strengths built into these formats.

Fourth, we introduce four steps to help you assemble, consolidate, and summarize your key competencies (also known as Knowledge, Skills, and Abilities—KSAs), documented results, career preferences, and the goals you've identified in the previous chapters. We'll weave in scripts to show you how to deliver the information in each of the four steps.

The Performance Review: A Main Event and More...

The performance review is certainly a main feature. But it's important to see the performance review as one step in an ongoing career process, not as an isolated event. A performance review is simply a marker along the way of an evolving, multifaceted, and continuing career path to tell you if you're on the mark and going in the right direction.

The "evaluation of your performance" starts the day you join the organization and continues with each project you do, every challenge you overcome, the opportunities you exploit, every skill you use, and the wealth of talents you exhibit.

The helpful feedback and input you get from the performance review can also help you to recover from the little (or big) career bloopers we all make along the way. It will help you chart a course for your career that will move it along more effectively. The performance review process tells **you** as much about your work and career as it does your manager.

That's why you don't want to see the performance review as an end in itself, but as an important step along your career path. Think of it as:

- **A checkpoint** to see where you are and how you're doing.

- **A heart monitor** to see if you're satisfied with your work and doing tasks and using skills that you enjoy.

- **A starting point** to go in a new direction with your job or career.

- **A rejuvenating tonic** to boost your enthusiasm for your work.

- **A reinforcement** to continue the path you are on in your organization and your career.

- **A learning alert** to assess your need to acquire more skills or knowledge, to keep you abreast of your career and in tune with the times.

- **A rich communication tool** for relaying your skills and accomplishments to those who need to know.

- **An "atta girl"** or **"atta boy"** that affirms your value to the organization and boosts your self-esteem.

"Rev-Up"- Activities to Do First

As we emphasized in the first chapter, Crash Course, a little preparation up front can save hours of frustration and angst. Here are some "rev-up" things you can do to insure the success of your performance review.

Get a heads up

Give yourself at least three months to get ready. Whoa, why three months? Long before the actual review takes place, the organization is acting on important information about you and making decisions that affect your future (such as compensation and promotions). You need to contribute any important information that will have a positive influence on those decisions, so start thinking "three months"!

Start with your job description

Thoroughly re-read your written job description. Document and be ready to present all the work you've done that's identified in your formal job description. Then be sure to include any responsibilities you've undertaken **beyond** the written job description. The Four Step Process found on page 79 will show you how to effectively communicate completed successes as well as projects still underway. Chapter 7 helps you deal with projects that encounter obstacles.

If you don't have a written job description, write a rough draft of one and give it to your manager for feedback. Make sure you and management are clear about the parameters of your job, as this will be the baseline against which they will evaluate you.

Get friendly with the performance review process and format

Take yourself down to the HR department and get a current copy of the performance appraisal form to see if it's changed. Be clear about what information the organization is trying to elicit from the performance review system. Check out the overall format, the definitions of the performance categories, rating scales, and if and how certain performance areas are weighted. The next section describes various performance appraisal formats, their pros and cons, and how to handle them.

Find out when performance reviews are done. Are they all done at once at the beginning or end of the year, or do they follow the employee's anniversary (date of hire) with the organization? If they are all done at the same time, expect to contend with your manager's heavy schedule.

Clarify the steps in the performance appraisal process outlined by your organization so you are clear about the time lines and your responsibilities. Most appraisal systems include a "self-evaluation" step, in which you assess your own performance before you meet with your manager. This is good news, because the organization has built in a perfect vehicle for you to apply all the preparation efforts we describe in this book.

Review your past performance reviews

Review your last year's goals and be prepared to discuss how you accomplished them. If you didn't meet some of your goals, be prepared to discuss why and what you are doing about it.

Prep your manager

Send your boss a bulleted list of your accomplishments and a progress report. Link this information to the broader organizational goals. Managers need this info in advance so they have time to act on it.

Prep for perks, salary, promotion

If negotiations for additional perks and salary or a promotion will be part of the review, be prepared with documentation as to why you deserve the increase or promotion. You'll find the techniques for amassing your accomplishments to document your value in Chapter 2 and the work you do telling your story; in Chapter 4, which talks about showing your effect on the bottom line; and in the Four Step Process on page 79.

Types of Performance Reviews and How to Handle Them

The formats used in performance appraisals fall into two major categories: 1) those more subjective elements that provide statements of, or require managers to write, performance, behaviors, attitudes, and results expected; and 2) the more objective evaluation criteria use a series of statements to describe levels of performance and/or numerical scales. The most common format is the blended, described on page 76.

Performance Behaviors

Most evaluations include sections with statements that describe the performance expected. These can take the form of:

Critical Competencies / KSAs

Critical competencies, or Knowledge, Skills, and Attitudes, are often customized for each job or job cluster. They identify critical behaviors required by the position and evaluate individuals according to the degree they do or do not exhibit these behaviors.

Example: Customer Service

Provides courteous and responsive customer support. Maintains rapport with customers, developing work relationships as required.

Example: Management

Demonstrates effective managerial skills in motivating and mentoring staff; provides feedback/coaching and timely performance evaluations.

Objectives / Management by Objectives

Objectives evaluate your performance against a pre-determined standard established in the previous review. Ideally, the objective will include a description of the task, behavior, or action required, the results expected, and a time frame.

Example:

> In the next 12 months [time frame] will continue to lead the region (result) in new product and program implementation for the research and reporting division [action, behavior, task].

Essay or Descriptive Section

An essay section usually provides the manager with a guided outline, or prompts, and requires the manager to produce a written description of the employee's performance.

Example:

What are the employee's major accomplishments?

What are the employee's best skills and how do they fit the position?

What skills, knowledge, or experience does the employee need to refine or acquire?

Evaluation Criteria

Standard appraisals usually include objective measures the manager can use to determine the employee's level of performance. They can take the form of:

Rating Scales

Example 1:
> 5 - Exceptional Performance
> 4 - Exceeds Expectations
> 3 - Meets Expectations
> 2 - Improvement Needed
> 1 - Unsatisfactory Performance

Example 2:

Rating	Points Available
Exceptional	85-97
Exceeds Expectations	72-84
Meets Expectations	50-71
Needs Development	<50

Forced Choice

Example:
> ___ Has a file labeled F and puts everything in it
> ___ Is extremely well organized

Yes/No

In some cases, the manager only has the option of indicating that the behavior exists or doesn't exist.

Example:

Result Achieved   Result Not Achieved

Ranking

Employees are compared to co-workers and rated according to their standing in the group.

Blended Formats

Most performance appraisals have a section combining these formats. The blended format allows for an objective analysis as well as an opportunity for the manager to flesh out in more detail the employee's performance behaviors. Some examples follow.

Example 1 uses objectives, statements that lay out what is to be done, when, and what results are expected, a section for comments, and a rating scale.

Objective:

Work with brand management and sales team to bring new xyz consumer product to market 2 months ahead of schedule.

Comments:

_____

_____

_____

_____

Exceptional Performance	Exceeds Expectations	Meets Expectations	Improvement Needed	Unsatisfactory Performance
❏	❏	❏	❏	❏

Example 2 uses critical competencies, also known as KSAs (Knowledge, Skills, and Attitudes), that describe critical behaviors required to do a job, plus a section for comments and a rating scale.

Knowledge, Skills, Abilities, and Other Characteristics

The items below describe the knowledge, skills, abilities and other characteristics an employee should exhibit in carrying out the essential function of his/her job. Read each section and comment on the extent to which the employee utilized that particular characteristic while performing his/her job, and rate the employee.

1. Quality of Work

Consider the quality of work produced, the thoroughness, neatness, accuracy and the promptness with which it is completed.

Comments:

_____

_____

_____

_____

Needs Improvement	Meets Expectations	Consistently High Quality
❏	❏	❏

Evaluation criterion in the form of rating scales, etc., although not foolproof, minimize subjectivity or bias, may give a specific indication of the "level" of performance, and show the relative gap between poor performance, desired performance, and excellent performance. However, scales and rankings give a very narrow and limited view of performance, and the simplistic rating may mask other good skills and successful efforts an employee has taken to bounce back from missteps or failures.

The essay and comment sections allow room for exceptions, explanations, enhancement, and causality. Like the essay exams in school that reveal what you **do** know, rather than what you don't know, the more subjective measures enable you to express what you **do** well and **enjoy** doing.

How to Handle Whatever Format Comes Your Way

As we mentioned in "Rev Up" for the performance review, it's important to get familiar with your organization's appraisal format so you can be as prepared as possible. You'll be able to take advantage of the opportunities provided in a well designed system and to counter any weaknesses inherent in an appraisal form that makes it difficult for you to communicate your value.

What do the rating categories really mean? For example, does "Exceptional Performance" in your organization signify "Close to God" and is it rarely given?

How complete are short statements that describe "Critical Competencies"? Do they adequately reflect what you really do and the results you achieved?

Do the objectives delineate what you do/did, the time line, and results?

Do forced choices, yes/no items, or rankings omit critical behaviors, skills, and accomplishments?

How to Compensate for / Take Advantage of Performance Review Elements

This is easy to do if you follow the Four Step Process we introduce in the next section of this chapter. The Four Step Process shows you how to develop narrative statements and bottom-line results to respond directly to items on the performance review or to enhance your responses in order to convey important information the structured format does not elicit.

Prepare for every performance review as if the format consisted of the essay, open-ended comments, and statements of objectives. The statements you develop allow you to fill in the gaps missed by the short answer, rating, forced choice, and ranking elements of the appraisal format. This preparation enables you to present and **prioritize** in person, or in writing, the accomplishments, talents, skills, and results that you want to convey to your boss. Preparing to report on objectives, whether they are ones already established in last year's review or new ones you've recently accomplished, drives home and expands the results you've achieved.

You can feel smug because you've already done most of this work in the previous chapters of this book. In the next section of this chapter we'll show you to take this valuable raw information and develop persuasive narratives and objectives you can present during your performance review.

Here are two examples to show you where we're going with all this.

Our previous example of Critical Competencies for a customer service position states:

> Provides courteous and responsive customer support. Maintains rapport with customers, developing work relationships as required.

In preparation for your review, you can elaborate on this statement to show your specific skills and results:

> *"I respond quickly and accurately to customer requests and complaints and establish good working relationships with them. I've tracked my calls for the last two months and discovered that I take approximately 30 calls a day. Given the average for the type of call I get, I turn them around in three minutes with good customer service. Over half the customers I deal with ask for me when they call again."*

Notice how this short narrative fills in the gaps in the example above: *"Quickly and accurately respond,"* *"Track my calls,"* and includes statements of results, *"Turn them around in three minutes"* and *"The majority of customers...ask for me when they call."*

Our other example of a Critical Competencies for management states:

> Demonstrates effective managerial skills in motivating and mentoring staff; provides feedback/coaching and timely performance evaluations.

You can extrapolate these competencies with this specific incident:

> *"Having worked extensively with the engineering department as well, I encouraged cross-functional teamwork. The benefit is not just to the department but to the company as a whole because it strengthens our effectiveness in the marketplace."*

Stick with us and we'll give you tips and scripts for preparing for your performance appraisal so words slip just this easily from your tongue.

Four Steps to Prepare for the Performance Review

Now that we've set the scene for the performance appraisal, let's get ready for the dress rehearsal. As we mentioned in Chapter 1, Crash Course, the form and formats of performance reviews will vary from organization to organization. In this chapter we've given you examples of various performance review elements that appear on traditional appraisal forms. Whatever the form, the information the appraisal system is designed to elicit is the same. Basically, management wants to know:

- What skills and knowledge you have and what you need to improve or acquire.
- How well you performed your tasks and responsibilities, and whether you met your goals set in last year's performance review.
- How you've grown and developed on the job.
- What job goals you have for the coming year.
- What long-term career goals you have identified.

The four steps presented below prepare you to perform well on any review, regardless of the form or format and the various performance review elements that may appear. Moreover, this preparation also greases the wheel for handling informal impromptu conversations as well. These steps are:

1. Profile your Knowledge, Skills, and Abilities (KSAs). (We include "Abilities" under Skills and Major Tasks, which follow.)

2. Profile your major tasks, projects, responsibilities, and results.

3. Describe your recent career growth and development.

4. Present your goals.

Much of the information you need to assemble here is already organized and waiting for you in the work you did in Chapters 2, 4, and 5.

Summary Form

Before we describe each step, here is an outline of the elements in the Four Step Process you can use to orient yourself as we wade into the details. This outline can also serve as a summary sheet to follow as you flesh out the four steps for your own performance review.

The Four Steps

Step 1 Profile your knowledge, skills, and abilities (KSAs)
- A. Skills
  1. Top Drawer
  2. Hot
  3. Touch Up
  4. Magnet
- B. Knowledge
  1. Top Drawer
  2. Hot
  3. Touch Up
  4. Magnet

Step 2 Profile your major tasks, projects, responsibilities, and results
- A. Name/brief description of the major task, project, or responsibility
- B. Why the effort was necessary
- C. What I did
- D. The results I achieved
- E. Performance against goals

Step 3 Recent Career Growth and Development
- A. On-the-job performance
- B. Personal development/personal management/career development

Step 4 Present career goals
- A. Stay where you are
- B. Enrich your job
- C. Move up or laterally
- D. Move down
- E. Move out
- F. What to do when you don't know where you want to go

STEP 1 - Key Competencies: Profile Your Skills, Knowledge, and Abilities

Key competencies, or KSAs, are the critical behaviors and skills needed to perform a job. Competencies are best described by technical, personal, and transferable skills. So this exercise to profile your skills and knowledge helps you to address the key competencies section of a performance review.

Most people facing a performance review emphasize the skills they need to improve or acquire. While it's important to look at limitations and develop new skills, particularly in today's fast changing job market, it's also important to **build from your strengths!**

When you operate on your best and most preferred skills, you fly through your work. You have more energy and more commitment to what you do. You're more creative and better able to handle problems when they come along. The fancy trappings of a career can't compensate for a job that requires you to constantly focus on your weaker skills. Even if you perform well, the struggle it takes to overcome these limitations eventually takes its toll on your energy, motivation, self-esteem, and productivity. Neither you nor the company benefits when you are mismatched to your best skills.

Inventory Your Skills:

Four categories of skills are listed here. We've included a sample list of skills to give you a jump-start. Borrow freely from these if they fit, and add your own.

Write them here or enter them in the organizational system we suggested in Chapter 2. After you've identified various categories of skills, you can focus on the ones you love to use!

Top-Drawer Skills: My best skills.

Hot Skills: The skills I possess which are most critical to the organization.

Touch-Up Skills: The skills I need to improve or acquire.

Magnet Skills: The skills I'm drawn to and love to use.

Sample List of Skills

Read people accurately	See a goal and develop steps to achieve it
Streamline systems	Defuse conflict
Calm angry customers	Organize information for easy retrieval
Listen attentively	Identify essential information
Problem-solve creatively	Attend to detail
Plan and organize	Manage events
Manage projects	Create order out of chaos
Create innovative solutions	Research
Find needed resources	Develop employees
Manage people	Connect with a wide variety of people
Train and teach	Advise, counsel, coach
Sell intangibles/tangibles	Promote ideas
Communicate complex ideas	Work with tools
Handle multiple tasks	Write clearly
Elicit sensitive information	Make process/systems better
Monitor and improve quality	Include outsiders
Give feedback tactfully	Mediate, find the middle ground
Negotiate	Answer questions
Fix machinery	Speak publicly
Arrange space efficiently	Manage facilities
Lead people to same goals	Get buy-in and support
Engender enthusiasm	Sing, dance, and play the piano

Scripts

Have some "skill language" ready to weave into your performance review. Here are some sample scripts.

My Top-Drawer Skills

"My best skills, the ones that underpin most of my successes, are my ability to lead a diverse team toward the same goals and develop specific steps to achieve a broad vision."

My Hot Skills

"The skills I bring which are most needed by the organization at this time are my abilites to negotiate contracts with our strategic partners and integrate different operational systems."

My Touch-Up Skills

"I would like to improve my time management skills, because I get too bogged down in details. I produce very accurate work, but I need help in setting priorities."

"I need to get certified on the next level of our software system if I am to stay current and work with some of the new clients we are acquiring."

"I think a class or some resources on how to delegate would help me be a better project manager."

My Magnet Skills

"I enjoy solving gnarly problems, such as how to reconfigure our offices to keep the same teams together when we relocate to the new building."

"I thrive on high-level negotiations when there is a lot at stake."

"I'm always striving to make data and people systems work together better. I just naturally gravitate to these kinds of situations."

Inventory Your Knowledge:

Now treat that valuable knowledge you have in your head the same as you did your skills. List your:

Top-Drawer Knowledge: Information I have that shows I am at the top of my game.

Hot Knowledge: The information I know that is most important to the organization.

Touch-Up Knowledge: Information I need to acquire or update.

Magnet Knowledge: The information I really enjoy having and using.

Here's a sample list of knowledge/information areas to give you a idea of what we mean by "knowledge areas." Add your own as needed.

ISO specifications	Contracts
Compliance rules	Building codes
Employment law	Cost accounting / tax law
CAD systems	Survey research techniques
Environmental issues	Medical billing processes
Principles of fundraising	Fiber optics
Public relations	Management theory

 Scripts

Top-Drawer Knowledge
"My knowledge of organizational effectiveness theory has enabled us to make important structural changes in our succession planning process."

Hot Knowledge
"My knowledge of the medical manufacturing and supply industries made it possible for us to diversify our plastic molding business and create new business during a downturn in our other enterprise centers."

Touch-Up Knowledge
"I would like to attend the Planned Giving Roundtable because it will help me determine if and how planned giving could be integrated into our development efforts."

"I need to learn more about the new employment laws that address people with disabilities."

"A class on market research techniques would enable me to do some research in-house, use fewer vendors, and do a better job of selecting vendors when we do need them."

Magnet Knowledge
"I like getting my teeth into the environmental issues and figuring out how we can comply and still save money."

Step 2 - Profile Your Major Tasks, Projects, Responsibilities, and Results

Your key responsibilities for the past year will be the centerpiece of your review. These surface in the performance review as objectives or competency statements. To recall the overwhelming number of tasks you performed during the year is daunting if you don't prepare for them in advance of going onstage. This section helps you mine your sterling accomplishments ahead of time so you can be ready with your lines when you're in the spotlight.

To make this task easy, refer back to Chapters 2 and 4. Information you need is found in 1) your Current Job, where you listed the best results you'd achieved for your organization; 2) your Work History; 3) Key Projects you completed; and 4) documenting the bottom line.

Here's a formula to use that makes it easy to select, mix, and match what you want to say. The format we use follows closely the format for writing objectives because we include what you did and the specific results you achieved. We'll provide examples so you see how easy it is to do.

1. Name/brief description of the major task, project, or responsibility.

2. Why the effort was necessary.
    (The organization's need or goal.)

3. What I did.
    (The responsibilities you had and the action you took.)

4. The results I achieved.
    (How your efforts benefited the organization/department, etc.)

5. Performance against goals.
    (Was this a pre-determined goal? If so, how did you perform against the goal?)

Here are two scripts that model what we mean. The first script is an administrative assistant in a mortgage bank who processes loan applications. The second script is a sales person who sells large, expensive presses to manufacturers.

Script #1

Major task, project, responsibility
"I created a system and checklist to proof loan applications for accuracy and completeness."

Why the effort was necessary
"Loans were taking too long to process because they had to be sent back to various departments for corrections or additional information."

What I did

"I created a system that included a checklist of items and a routing sheet that each person in the process had to follow. It was computerized for easy access and also available in a hard copy that could be attached to the top of the packet."

Results I achieved

"We not only cut the time in half to process the papers, but also reduced the number of errors, the time it took to correct the errors, and the needless re-contacting of the customer."

Was this a pre-determined goal? If yes, how did I perform against the goal?

"Workflow/efficiency is one item in the performance review on which each employee is evaluated. This demonstrates my ability to analyze systems for efficient and effective workflow."

Script #2

In this script we put all the parts together to show how smoothly your lines can flow when you're prepared.

Activity: Generated additional income for company by convincing clients who wouldn't buy new tablet press machinery to pay for reconditioning of their old presses.

"I recognized we were missing out on revenue that our competitors were generating, by not getting some kind of business from clients who wouldn't buy new presses. I arranged with our repair department, whose only job was to repair clients' presses when they broke down, to submit proposals for reconditioning used machinery that could be sold to new or existing customers. The client would save the cost of a new machine, we would still gain revenue, and the repair department would become a revenue-generating entity. By re-conditioning presses for current, as well as new, clients, we generated $100,000 of revenue in eight months that otherwise would have been lost. The $100,000 in new revenue helped me surpass my annual sales goal two months prior to the end of the year."

Step 3 - Describe Your Recent Career Growth and Development

This step helps you communicate how you are developing, growing, and staying current in changing times. Your professional growth is usually an important part of a performance review, but it can hold an important place in a career conversation as well. Step 3 breaks down into two categories.

1. **On-the-job performance**
   (Job-specific skills, knowledge, experience you acquire)
2. **Personal development/personal management/career development**
   (Personal and career skills you develop that support and enhance your work with the organization—for example, time management, organizational skills, communication skills, self-assessment experiences)

Here are two scripts that model what we mean. Once again we use the examples of our administrative assistant in the mortgage bank and our machinery salesman.

Script #1

1. On-the-job performance

"I've been talking to other people involved in the generation and processing of loans to learn all I can about our organization and the systems we use. I've talked to two or three people a month for the last three or four months. These discussions helped me develop the review packet that reduced loan processing time and errors. I also try to read and comprehend a lot of the information that comes across my desk, even if it doesn't relate directly to my job. In fact many times I use my lunch hour for this. I'm finding it helps me better understand the organization, what we do, and how we do it."

2. Personal development/personal management/ career development

"I know there are many different kinds of positions in this company. I'm keeping a record of what I do, what I like, and what I'm best at so I can do a better job of finding my next position here. As I've discussed with you before, I would eventually like to move up, out of administrative/clerical. Keeping track of my work progress and preferences will help me target other positions that would be a good match of my talent and skills and make me valuable to the organization."

Script #2

1. On-the-job performance

"Last year I took some classes on sales techniques, which the organization paid for. This year I have been implementing what I learned. I learned how to be more effective at consultative sales, something I gravitate to naturally. The class, however, not only gave me more techniques, but also reinforced what I was already doing well. I have really established good relationships with customers. And I'm confident those who haven't already purchased more from me will in the next year to year and a half. I think my skill development is reflected in the fact that I've already exceeded my goals, and the year isn't over yet."

2. Personal development/personal management/ career development

"I think a lot of our success in sales depends on some good marketing techniques. Since we don't have a large marketing department, I've been reading about marketing and basic business communication skills, including writing. It's been a real help to my sales efforts."

Step 4 - Present Your Goals

Now you are ready to prepare your script and present your career goals. In the last chapter we reviewed these options:

Option 1 Stay where you are

Option 2 Stay where you are and enrich the job you have

Option 3 Move upward

Option 4 Move laterally to a new function

Option 5 Move downward

Option 6 Move out

Option 7 Explore, when you don't know what you want

As you can see from Option 7, we'll also discuss how to handle a performance review or career conversation when you know you need a change, but you don't know what you want. To prepare for any of the options, you will be drawing, again, on your key skills, accomplishments, and experiences that you detailed in Chapters 2, 4, and 5. If you haven't visited those chapters for a while, a quick review will help.

Option 1 – Stay Where You Are

Staying where you are is usually the easiest choice for everyone involved. But remember, you don't want to mark time, even though you're not moving up, over, or out. You'll want to remind management that your skills and knowledge are current and your work is vital to the organization. Be prepared to discuss:

- Why you want to remain in your current position and how this decision benefits you and the organization.

- What you want to achieve in the coming year.

- Your plans for achieving your goals.

- The additional help or resources you need from your manager/ department/organization.

Here are two scripts that model what we mean. Our administrative assistant and salesperson re-appear.

Script #1

Why you want to remain in your current position and how this decision benefits you and the organization

"I would like to remain in this position because I'm still learning about the position and the company. At some time in the future I will want to move up to a more responsible position, but doing a good job here will prepare me for the move. This position allows me to interact with many other departments, if I take the initiative— which I do. This helps me do my current job better and target a future position in the organization. Although I'm still learning, I do a good job for the organization. I complete my work accurately and on time. I have been increasing my productivity every month—getting out more applications. And I know enough about the position that I can make modifications and changes to improve systems and workflow, which I enjoy."

What you want to achieve in the coming year

"In the coming year I would like to improve my productivity by 30% and tackle the process by which we communicate to our clients the status of their loan—where it is in the process. Obviously I cannot communicate the legal and technical information about their loan, but we can do a better job of keeping in touch with clients about the progress. I have a few ideas about ways we could increase the contact and improve client relations."

Your plans for achieving your goals

"To improve my productivity, I need to become more familiar with two other departments. I will make appointments to talk to people in those departments to learn more specifically what they want to see and how they want to see it. Learning this will help me process my work faster. I'm also in the process of writing down some ideas for customer communication. Next month I'd like to run my ideas by you to see if you think they would work. Finally, I would like to take some finance courses that would be appropriate for my level."

What additional help or resources you need from your manager/ department/organization

"Could you suggest a financial class I could take that would help me understand the loan and mortgage business? And do you know other people in the organization I could call to help me understand how my work relates to other functions in the organization? I have a list here of people I've seen and those I'm planning to contact, but I could use some suggestions from you."

Script # 2

Why you want to remain in your current position and how this decision benefits you and the organization

"I really like what I do and I'm making good progress with my customers. I've exceeded my goals, and I would like to look at other ways to generate sales, such as selling reconditioned machines to customers and prospects who won't buy new ones. I have developed a loyal following for our organization and want to capitalize on that for us."

What you want to achieve in the coming year

"I want to exceed the sales I've made this year by 40-50%, which will be considerable, since I've exceeded this year's goals by $75,000. I'd like to look for other ways to generate revenue in addition to new equipment sales, and I'd like to expand our market to at least six other nutrition, vitamin, and pharmaceutical companies who use our type of presses. I think we could be more aggressive."

Your plans for achieving your goals

"I attended an industry conference and obtained a valuable mailing list of attendees. I plan to select the companies who could use our equipment and systematically contact them. I figure there are about 35 prospect companies on that list. I also think we could make more money on our repair contracts, particularly if we promote it correctly and add a few low-cost bells and whistles. I'll continue to call on my customers. I usually contact them every couple of months, but I'm going to up that to every month."

Option 2—Enrich the Job You Have

If you like your present position but need some new stimulation and change, you may want to enrich your job. Turn to Chapter 5 if you need a refresher on ways you can enhance your current work. If job enrichment is your career choice, be prepared to discuss:

- How you want to enrich your job.

- How this benefits you and the organization.

- The skills, knowledge, and experience you already have to help you.

- Additional resources you need to help you achieve your goals.

- How your manager/organization can help.

Here are two scripts that model what we mean. This first script is a human resource specialist who does recruiting and training. The second script is a training person who developed an orientation program for new hires.

Script #1

How you want to enrich your job

"In addition to recruiting, I'd like to work on more training, particularly in the area of diversity. I'd like to minimize the work I do on training support. Joe, who is in training support, would like to expand his job, and I think he could pick up my extra work so I could focus on training, diversity, and recruiting."

How this benefits you and the organization

"We have diversity in our strategic plan and mission statement, but no single person is taking responsibility for it. I would like to work into that position. I can continue to do my job in recruiting and have the satisfaction and excitement of working on a new project I believe in."

The skills, knowledge, and experience you already have to help you

"I have been studying diversity and recruiting. I've developed skills and knowledge through my interaction with the professional group. I already know the organization, the possibilities, and a lot of the players."

Additional resources you need to help you

"I need your support and that of upper management to do this, and I would like assistance in setting appropriate goals for diversity. I'd also like to sit on a company-wide committee where diversity could be represented. Do you know of any such committee?"

Script #2

How you want to enrich your job

"I'm enjoying platform training and orientation, but would like to expand the courses I could develop to include work/life balance, time management, and attitude adjustment. In addition, I'd like to see if I could work on a project with human resources so I learn more about their functions. Perhaps they'd like me to develop a course for them. I could interview them, do my own research, and call some people in my professional association who would have helpful information."

How this benefits you and the organization

"Expanding my content area makes me more valuable to the organization. Our last employee survey indicated some morale problems. I think a course on work/life balance and attitude adjustment would help, particularly in light of new national and international events that have everyone concerned. And most everyone needs help with time management. It's a good companion to work/life balance, as well. I'd like to work with HR because I think the training and HR could do a better job of linking and cooperating. It's not that they don't want to, but everyone is very busy, and I think I have the time and energy to be a liaison between the two departments."

The skills, knowledge, and experience you already have to help you

"I had not done an orientation program before, so I studied the programs of other companies, learned what I needed to know, and developed the orientation program from scratch. So I know how to research a new area and develop a training course on it."

Additional resources you need to help you achieve your goals

"I want to read and study work/life balance, time management, and attitude adjustment issues and programs. I have two books on attitude. A colleague I met at our professional association has done a "positive attitude" program in his organization that has been very successful, and he offered to help me. I have sent for literature from the Work Life Balance Roundtable at Boston College that has helpful information for developing such programs. I took a great time management class in college. The professor was excellent, and he said he would share some of his materials with me.

I talked to some folks from HR when I was in the cafeteria last week. They said they'd be happy to talk to me about what they do. I'm going to make an appointment to see them before or after work one day this month. I've attended some of the orientation workshops they've held on benefits, etc. just to see who they are and what they do."

How your manager/organization can help

"I need your feedback on these goals to see if I'm being realistic. I would appreciate any resources you can think of in the area of positive attitude, time management, and work/life balance. Can you suggest anyone in HR I could talk to that you think would help me or be interested in a joint project?"

Options 3 & 4—Move Up or Move Laterally

A lateral or upward move is a more dramatic career decision. You will need to develop a compelling rationale to convince management that this is the move you should make. Put special emphasis on how the organization would benefit from this change. Be prepared to discuss:

- The position(s) that interest you.

- What you've done to research the position, and why it would be a good career move.

- How you and the organization would benefit from this move.

- The job-specific skills, knowledge, and experiences you would bring to the position.

- Other skills, knowledge, and experiences that would transfer to the position.

- The skills, knowledge, and experiences you would need to refine or acquire in order to move into this position.

- Obstacles or advantages that would influence your move into this position (organizational norms, location, etc.).

- Your time frame for making the move.

Here are two scripts to model what we mean—one for moving up and one for moving laterally.

Script #1

The position that interests you / Your research / Why it would be a good career decision

"I would like to move up to the next level of management, either in this department, since it's been announced that there may a position available, or some other part of the organization that would use my management skills and company knowledge. I've been with the organization for nine years and am very familiar with our inner workings, particularly customer interface regarding quality care and service."

How the organization would benefit

"This organization would benefit from my company knowledge and my management skills. Our strategic plan states that the development of management and leadership skills is a priority, and I bring those skills to any position I hold. This position is no longer tapping the additional, higher-level skills I possess. I'm grooming people who could take over this position, and I believe the organization would benefit from moving me to another position where I could use my higher-level

skills to generate revenue, improve customer service, and reduce complaints and regulatory problems."

The job-specific skills that would transfer to this position

"I already have the management skills. As you know, I expanded the department 30% and initiated a new, successful team management approach. One of my best skills is instituting new management structures and forming cohesive work groups. A promotion to another level of management would enable me to not only do this, but also train other managers in this kind of leadership development."

Other skills, knowledge, and experiences that would transfer to the position

"I have a lot of information about our competitors. It came out of the survey work I did. This will be a great benefit in the next position, not to mention the knowledge I have about our organization. My ability to develop a cohesive department and work well with other units will be an asset in the next position."

Skills/Knowledge you would need to refine or acquire

"I have the management skills, but I need to familiarize myself with our large accounts. I am already doing research on them, so I can hit the ground running when I move up."

Other Obstacles/Advantages

"We've had some senior level people retire or leave, and I feel I could help fill a gap. The hiring and promotion freeze should be over by the time I'm ready to move."

Time Frame

"As far as preparation is concerned, I'm ready to move now. But I think it would be best if I finish the current large-scale initiative I'm directing and hand that over completed to my replacement. That will take another three months."

Script #2

The position that interests you

"I'd like to move into a marketing role for our environmental engineering division and make that my sole responsibility."

How you and the organization would benefit

"I have the operations/business administration side running smoothly, and Sandra or Tom could easily assume my position, so I wouldn't leave a gap. The environmental side of our business is growing, but it could provide a larger percentage of our revenue if we seriously mar-

keted it. Right now it shares marketing with all the other divisions. I have figured the increase in revenue would justify the slight increase in pay that Sandra or Tom would need to assume my position."

The job-specific skills, knowledge, and experiences you would bring to the position

"As I mentioned before, I have been taking classes on marketing for technical professionals and have some business development strategies that are low or no cost, except for my time. In fact, I instituted one of them—the tour of client facilities. I have visited PEMA—the Professional Environmental Marketing Association—and have begun to make some good contacts there. I have good people skills and it's easy for me to meet new people. My business administration skills and computer knowledge make it easy for me to keep a prospect database and do consistent follow-up with prospects and current clients."

Other skills, knowledge, and experiences that would transfer to the position

"My tenure with our organization and my work in business administration have given me lots of exposure to the project managers and clients. I think the project managers need help with business development. I could not only do business development myself but also help and support the business development efforts of the project managers who are more technically inclined. You get double benefit in business development—a person to focus on it and an increase in the business development efforts of your project managers. In addition, I could serve in a client relations role at the same time, give clients TLC, identify problems, and route them to the right person to get the problems solved."

Skills and knowledge you need to refine or acquire

"I already mentioned that I'm taking classes in marketing for technical organizations. I'm also signing up for a class on web design. Although I won't have the high level skills to do our web page the way we want it, I will gain knowledge to help me select a vendor and oversee the project."

Other obstacles or advantages

"I need to convince Sandra or Tom to take over my current position, and I think that's doable. Also, I'll need to convince the organization as a whole that marketing is a necessary and critical function to our healthy survival."

Time Frame

"I can begin transitioning now and have marketing as my sole responsibility by the end of the year."

Option 5–The Stress-Saver Move Down

If you're considering a move down, figure out where you want to go. Is your goal a position you've held before, or a new one? If you're not sure, use the strategies introduced in Chapter 5 to help you.

Your desire to move down increases your need to prepare for your career encounter. Use the four-step preparation model to prove your value to the organization. Demonstrating your commitment and desire to contribute will help you enlist the wholehearted support of your organization for this less-than-common career move.

So, follow the preparation model: Present your skills. Profile your major tasks and accomplishments. Describe your recent career growth. And be prepared to discuss:

- Why you want to move down (keep it positive).

- How the organization will benefit.

- Your commitment to the organization and your career.

Here are two scripts to model what we mean.

**Script #1**

Why you want to move down
"My year has gone well. I've met my goals and the department has met its goals. But I feel this position does not draw on my best skills. I struggle to coordinate and organize the staff, which I do. The job gets done, no doubt about it. But my ability to analyze data, see trends, and identify problems is not being tapped in this position. I'd like to return to my former position that gave me great latitude to use these skills. I can do this data analysis with half my brain tied behind my back."

How the organization would benefit
"I work long and hard at my current job, but I would be a more productive worker for you in my former function because the work comes more naturally to me, and I like to solve the kinds of problems that arise in that role. I know my former position has not been replaced with anyone at my level of experience, so I believe I can help that department be more productive and cutting edge. You have other staff, skilled at people and project management, who could step into my role here. And I don't mind taking the salary cut that comes with the former position."

Your commitment to the organization and your career

"I like it here and I want to be sure I'm making the best contribution I can to the organization. I think moving me to my former position is in the best interest of the organization, and it is a better fit for my skills and career goals."

Script #2

Why you want to move down

"As I've mentioned before, this department requires the production of a lot of information that has to be absolutely accurate and produced at breakneck speed. I do the work, and my performance reviews indicate I work at and above average. I believe, however, that my best skills are used when I interface with people and handle their problems. This can be fast-paced as well, but the pace when I'm dealing face to face or on the phone with people seems challenging and exciting, not draining. I would like to move to a position in customer service. Even though it is a step down for me, I believe it is a better fit for my skills and personality."

How the organization would benefit

"I've done some research. I know we are short-staffed in customer service, and turnover is high. I think I can make a real contribution to the organization by being in that department. Not only is the customer contact a good fit for my skills, but also I think I can bring some teamwork to the group. That was one of the contributions I made in this department, as you noted on my last performance review."

Your commitment to the organization and your career

"I want to be an enthusiastic and productive employee. I'm enthusiastic about the organization, and I think I can be a great producer and make more of a contribution in this area of the company that has some challenges. I'm intrigued with customer service and am considering attending ICSA—the International Customer Service Association. I'd like to re-direct my career toward customer service/ client relations. I believe I can prove myself in customer service, and I will be able to make up for this temporary backward move."

Option 6–Move Out

Some organizations conduct "exit" interviews to discover why employees leave. Below is a script that models how you can present both positive information and constructive criticism. If your organization doesn't offer an exit interview, you may find an opportunity to speak informally with management about your decision.

Keeping in mind that you don't want to burn bridges, here are things you may want to discuss as you tell management that you are leaving the organization:

- Why you need to leave.

- What you've gained while working for the organization.

- What you feel you've contributed.

- What the organization did that helped you do your job.

- What conditions or circumstances could have been different or improved that would have made your job more efficient, effective, or easier.

- To what degree and how you'd like to keep in touch.

When you need to leave your organization, use the following scripts as models to exit on a positive note.

Script #1

Why you need to leave
"I have explored my options in the organization and see that there is nowhere for me to go in my present position. I don't want to transfer to another department, and there isn't any opportunity for me to advance here."

What you've gained while working for the organization
"I've learned a great deal about the industry and the operations of the organization. I've developed skill and knowledge in operations and business management. I need to move to a position where I have more responsibility."

What you feel you've contributed
"I have streamlined and improved the business operations, including installing a software system for accounting and client tracking. I've attracted some talented people to the department and trained them well."

What the organization did that helped you do your job
"The organization was very good about paying for training on the computer systems and management and leadership. The training and support of the organization helped me grow in my job. I met some very talented people here whom I will continue to see after I leave."

What conditions or circumstances could have been different or improved that would have made your job more efficient, effective, or easier

"If the organization would put more emphasis on internal promotion and using talent they already have, they would save some good people they lose. At times, the goals could have been more clearly identified and communicated. Sometimes I felt I was working in the dark when it came to the outcomes that were expected of me."

To what degree and how you'd like to keep in touch

"As I mentioned, I've really enjoyed the people in the organization and will keep in touch. Please feel free to call on me if you need any information or resources I have that would be helpful to the organization."

Script #2

Why you need to leave

"My working style and philosophy for dealing with customers and co-worker differs from that of this culture. The organization wants us to be assertive and short-term in our approach to prospective clients and monitors us to do a great many cold calls each day. My style is to build relationships over time and visit people in person. It takes longer to get initial sales, but I easily catch up and meet or exceed goals at the end of the year. However, I understand why the company has this philosophy and that many people are successful using the company's techniques as witnessed by the organization's continuing success. I feel, however, that both the company and I will be better served if I move to an organization with a more compatible style to mine."

What you've gained from working with the organization

"I've learned a lot about sales. The sales training was invaluable, particularly the class on consultive sales. I've had the opportunity to work with some top-notch people with whom I hope to keep in touch."

What you feel you've contributed

"I was always a motivated and enthusiastic employee. I penetrated an industry the company had not served in the past. I supported new sales people and tried to help them acclimate to the new culture."

What the organization did that helped you do your job

"The weekly reports and monthly meetings helped keep me on track and kept me abreast of what was happening in the company. I appreciated that."

What conditions or circumstances could have been different or improved that would have made you job more efficient, effective, or easier

"Allowing for more individual style might generate more productivity from your employees. If the company had set six- and nine-month goals for me, I believe I would have proved that my style is successful and generates results over time."

To what degree and how you'd like to keep in touch

"I will stay in touch with my sales team. And if I can help you with information or resources in any way, please let me know."

Option 7–When You Don't Know What You Want

Are you searching for a role in the organization, but don't yet know where you fit? Once again, check out Chapter 5 for suggestions on how to explore your options. In the meantime, here's how to present your current undecided state to management so they will take you seriously. Be prepared to discuss:

- Your best experiences and accomplishments since you've been with the organization.

- Your "hot" skills and your "magnet" skills (those skills that are most needed by the organization and those you most enjoy using).

- Your general career interests, needs, and goals: what you want from work. (Chapter 2 captures this critical information.)

- The actions you are taking to explore your environment, learn about the organization, and uncover possible career options.

- How to transition out of your current position in a way that does not compromise the department/unit, etc.; how it can benefit you and the organization.

- The help you need to find your best place in the organization (suggestions, resources, people to talk with, training, etc.).

Here are scripts to model what we mean.

 **Script #1**

Your best skills and accomplishments since you've been with the organization

"I've enjoyed purchasing. I've learned a lot and have been able to expand my job until I can't expand it any more. I helped bring in and

mastered our just-in-time software. I've changed vendors and re-negotiated contracts to save us over $100,000 in the past two years. I've developed and streamlined systems in my area of purchasing so the function runs very smoothly with very few glitches. The staff I supervise is happy and productive. I'm at the point in my career here where I need to find more challenging work in the organization."

Your "hot" skills and your "magnet" skills (those skills that are most needed by the organization and those you most enjoy using)
"One of my best skills that I would like to maximize is my ability to see new revenue-generating opportunities. As a computer distributor our success depends on finding new, hot, innovative products we can purchase cost-effectively and sell to a hungry market. I was responsible for identifying and suggesting we purchase our last line of computer support equipment, which has been very successful."

Your general career interests, needs, and goals: what you want from work
"Procuring the computer support equipment was a related activity, because it involved purchasing. But the research and identification of the line was an expansion of my job. This activity, however, gave me a great deal of satisfaction and was beneficial for the company. I'd like to find a position in the organization that would use these skills. I like work that gives me contact with people outside of the organization. And I feel a greater sense of accomplishment when I do something new or innovative that contributes to the bottom line."

The actions you are taking to explore your environment, learn about the organization, and uncover possible career options
"Because I like to work with people outside of the organization, I've been talking to people in marketing and public affairs. Marketing feels closer to what I like to do – but not exactly. I've attended the American Marketing Association and Public Relations Society of America. I would enjoy dealing with current clients and customers, but still feel I want a challenge to help the organization look at new things."

The help you need to find your best place in the organization (suggestions, resources, people to talk with, training, etc.)
"Can you suggest other people I could talk to inside the organization? Would you suggest I talk to the sales department? I'm not sure sales is exactly it, but I have a sense I need to at least talk to them. Do you agree? Do you know of any other associations I could attend or resources I could read?"

Not every performance will be award winning. Now that you know how to handle the performance review under ideal situations, let's discuss what to do when your performance appraisal process hits a snag. Perhaps you came to the review with insufficient rehearsals and without knowing your lines. Or you simply didn't perform to expectations. Maybe you were the victim of a less than competent or irascible manager. Whatever the reason, you need to know how to handle a bad review. Chapter 7 will coach you.

7

Dealing with an Imperfect Performance

How do you take charge when your performance appraisal process hits a brick wall? What happens if you can't get your manager to give you a performance evaluation, or you get a poor one that accurately zeros in on problems, or a weak evaluation you feel isn't deserved? It's critical to your career that you have consistent evaluations and that you restore your reputation with the organization if you receive a poor one. Let's examine some of the obstacles and problems you can encounter in the performance appraisal process and what you can do about them.

Your Manager Stonewalls Your Review

Discomfort, an overwhelming workload, lack of skill, and fear are reasons managers will unduly delay or ignore giving you your performance review. Your first reaction may be "Whew, dodged that bullet! Don't have to worry about that." But beware. Just because you are not formally evaluated doesn't mean that your performance is not being judged. People (including management) are critiquing you everyday—your image, behavior, working style, habits, perceived accomplishments or lack of them. The good news about a performance review is that the evaluation of you is out in the open, and you have a fighting chance to make a good impression or counter a bad one.

Evaluation-by-default is risky. Moving along in your career without clear expectations, feedback, or recognition of your status leaves you open to unwarranted criticism and consequences. If you're struggling on the job, it allows you to continue to under-perform or fail without the opportunity to make good, and can lead to the demise of your career with that organization. A head-in-the-sand approach allows good work and achievements to go unnoticed or to be attributed to other people or factors. It may mask differences in style and personality with your manager, department, or organization that can lead to conflicts and misunderstandings and create unwarranted, negative impressions about your skills, attitude, or performance.

Pull your head out of the sand (if it's stuck there) and take charge of your own evaluation if your manager won't. How do you do that? Read on.

1. Read your manager

Before you charge ahead, take stock of your manager's style and the current business conditions your manager and organization may be facing. How does she like to communicate? What are her hot buttons? What business challenges are facing her that will affect her receptiveness, or lack of it, to your approach? Chapter 8 includes detailed lists to help you analyze your manager's working and communication styles.

Key into the manager's deliverables, those goals and objectives for which she's accountable. Your help with her deliverables will give you leverage in asking for a review. Your chance of success in pushing for your performance review will be greater if you figure out the best way and the most opportune time to approach your manager.

2. Do your homework

Even though your manager is stalling on your appraisal appointment, prepare for your performance review as if you were going to walk onstage tomorrow. With the techniques outlined in this book, you have the tools to do just that.

3. Ask your manager for a review

Approach your manager about holding a performance review in the manner you've determined will be the most effective.

Now's a good time to introduce (or re-introduce) your bulleted list of accomplishments we mentioned in the "Rev Up" section of Chapter 6. One of our scripts below shows you how to use the list as an opener for your request.

Ask to speak to your manager after a meeting and make the request at that time.

Set a short meeting with your boss. Ask for a performance review and request a specific date.

Send a memo, written tactfully, requesting a review. This can be your first attempt if your boss prefers written communication, or it can be a technique you use when the in-person attempts described above don't work.

Here are some ways to phrase a request for a performance review:

Scripts

"Chris, I notice it's time for my performance appraisal. I've compiled for you a list of my skills, projects, accomplishments, and how they link to the organization's goals. Do you need anything else from me to get my performance review prepared? And what date do you have in mind?"

"Chris, I notice my performance review is past due. I need some feedback on my progress and a couple of the larger responsibilities I've undertaken in the past year and the role they'll play for you, the department, and me this coming year. Could we schedule some time for a review in the next several weeks?"

"Chris, I haven't had a performance review for 18 months. My projects are going well—on time and under budget—but I don't have a feel for how the organization views my progress. Could we schedule a review in the next couple of weeks?"

"Chris, I've completed the objectives we established at my last performance review 16 months ago. Most of my major tasks are drawing to a close. I'd like to schedule a performance review to check on my progress and set new objectives that will be in line with your needs and goals and the goals of the organization. Is it possible to schedule the performance review sometime during the next three weeks?"

More Stonewalling? Review Yourself

What if your manager continues to ignore or delay your review? It may seem impossible after that compelling request—but it happens.

The techniques you use to conduct an effective performance review are not unlike those you use to handle an effective job interview. Coaches will advise you to prepare questions and answers in advance of an interview. Not only are you better prepared to answer the questions the interviewer asks, but also you can simply interview yourself if you encounter a poor interviewer.

So, if all attempts to get your manager to conduct your performance review fail, take the extreme step and—review yourself. You may feel your bulleted list of accomplishments is sufficient, or you can prepare a more complete overview and evaluation of your work efforts and performance.

Follow the organization's format if they have one, or construct your own from the suggestions we've provided here. Put your self-review in writing and be sure to include any of the following that apply to your situation. These will sound familiar because you've just completed detailing them in Chapter 6.

- The key competencies or Knowledge, Skills, and Abilities required for your job and the degree to which you meet these competencies or possess the KSAs. If your organization doesn't delineate them, create them from your own experience in the position.

- Major tasks and projects completed (objectives you established in last year's review and new ones you've established and met).

- The results you've achieved and the effect on the bottom line whenever possible.

- Your best skills and qualities if they are not already covered in the key competencies section.

- Goals and objectives for next year; areas in which you want to grow and develop.

- Whatever help you need to accomplish your goals and develop in your job.

This activity may require very little effort if you've done the previous work in this book. Your self-review can be a few pages or a short summary. As always, pick the method that will be best received by your manager.

What do You do With This Masterpiece?

What you do with this review will depend on your particular situation. If your relationship with your boss is tenuous and you suspect his motives, it may be prudent to leave your self-review in your desk drawer, ready to use as documentation if a problem arises or other higher ups in the organization develop an interest in you and your performance.

You may feel very comfortable delivering your self-review to your manager if you believe he is well meaning, cooperative, and amenable to your taking charge. He may welcome your efforts if he is simply too busy, feeling overwhelmed, or intimidated by the appraisal process to take the initiative himself.

When you present your self-review, ask your manager to give you feedback after he's had a chance to review it. This is a sure cure for the manager who delays a performance review because he is overwhelmed with work. Reading and responding to information is much easier than generating information.

You can deliver it in person and simply go over it face-to-face, leaving the written document behind like a calling card for your manager to review later.

Deliver it ahead of time so your manager has time to review it before you meet.

Any reasonable, well-meaning manager should not be offended by a tactfully executed strategy such as we suggest here. In fact, she should welcome it. If you feel anxious about your manager's reaction to the strategies and techniques suggested in this book, it may be a signal that there is a serious problem between you and your boss, one that has probably festered for a long time and may not be fixable.

Before you jump to that serious conclusion, be sure you've looked at the situation from both sides of the desk and tried to understand your manager's personality, style, and current challenges. If the situation still seems hopeless, you may need to take a long, hard look at your current position and consider whether or not you need to explore other options inside or outside of your organization. Although it feels easier to put off the inevitable, it's not wise, and it makes the situation more difficult to rectify in the long term. As the old saying goes, "The sooner you nip a problem in the bud, the easier it is to solve it."

> Marilyn, who worked for a civil environmental engineering firm as a project manager and marketer, was constantly lauded by her company for her good work, but hadn't received a performance review for two years. After making many requests that were ignored, she wrote a document that listed her major responsibilities and achievements, and included positive comments she'd received from her manager, co-workers, and clients. She presented it to her manager and asked if he would sign it and place it in her file. He did, and both heaved a sigh of relief—the manager because he didn't have to do a review and Marilyn because she had documentation in her file about her good work.

How to Rebound From a Bad or Mediocre Review

Every actor at some point in his career has awakened the morning after a premier performance to read a curdling review in the paper. Whether it's deserved or not, dedicated actors take action to reclaim their reputation rather than marinate in the sour aftermath of the critics' stinging words. Likewise, almost every employee, at some point in his or her career, has to deal with a distasteful performance review. It might be a failure, a missed opportunity, or a critical lapse in performance.

One of the most important career survival skills you can learn is how to rehabilitate yourself after a setback. Almost more important is the need for you to reclaim your own self-worth after a "one-two" punch to your ego, because without your self-esteem intact it's difficult to marshal the will and the energy needed to bounce back. So what can you do when you receive a bad or less than glowing performance review, and, unhappily, it's accurate?

Acknowledge it

Admit to yourself that you blundered, but don't beat yourself up emotionally, because the negativity will stall your recovery and degenerate into inertia. The sooner you begin re-structuring after a setback (assuming you've accurately figured out the problem), the sooner you'll get back on track.

Pinpoint the problem

Determine why you suffered this setback so you can get busy fixing it. Some reasons may be that you:

- Are mismatched to your job and required to use skills that are your weakest or less preferred.

- Are partially mismatched to your job. Many responsibilities you have may be in your area of strength, but one or two are torpedoing an otherwise sterling performance.

- Are mismatched to the organization.

- Need training to build skills, knowledge, or experience that will help you excel.

- Are distracted by personal problems or other work priorities.

- Feel overwhelmed by your workload.

- Were unaware of the importance of the tasks in question.

- Were unclear about established expectations, or priorities that have since evolved and changed.

- Were simply lackadaisical or too casual about your responsibilities.

- Need an attitude adjustment because your negative outlook affects your performance and/or interaction with others.

Determine if it's fixable

It's important to ascertain if the organization will give you the opportunity to correct the situation. Unless this is one in a series of warnings you've received, you probably will have a chance to fix the problem(s). Ask your manager for guidelines and the goals you must achieve to improve your performance.

Develop a plan to FIX IT

Develop a response and a plan of action to improve your performance. Present it to your manager and get his consensus that you are attacking the right problem(s) and doing so in the right way. Depending on the nature of the problems, your plan could include the need to:

- Acquire needed skills, experience, or knowledge.

- Seek additional training formally or informally.

- Get help with distractions from a coach, counselor, advisor, a family pow wow.

- Clarify on an ongoing basis your manager's expectations and priorities.

- Recommit yourself to personal excellence and a good work ethic and specify what this means (getting to work on time, getting tasks done when required, following through, etc.).

- Seek other help, if needed, from your human resources representative, a colleague, a co-worker, a coach, mentor, or counselor.

- Reconfigure your job to better match your skills, experience, and talents.

- Consider a different position to better suit your skills, experience, and talents.

Quick-start your performance

It is critical after a poor evaluation to demonstrate excellent performance as quickly as possible. Start with an easy task that yields fast results you can show to your manager. Lay down a new foundation as fast as possible to prove to your manager that you're taking the review seriously and are committed to change and improvement. In other words, start re-programming your manager's image of you, so that he sees a committed worker who learns from mistakes, bounces back from adversity, and demonstrates high-octane performance.

Keep in touch

When your performance evaluation is tenuous, do not let weeks or months fly by without getting periodic updates on your performance, particularly when you are doing well and recouping from your past blunder. Keep in touch with your manager to review your progress on an ongoing basis, whether it's weekly, biweekly, or monthly.

How to Handle a Bad Review You Don't Deserve

It's devastating to receive a bad, or even mediocre, performance evaluation when you feel you don't deserve it. As with the bad review we discussed above, it's important to rebound and restructure as soon as possible. Many of the techniques and suggestions we presented before apply here, the first being to figure out what went wrong and why.

No fault, no blame

Avoid the "blame game" – starting with yourself. Give yourself a break because you deserve one, and persisting in self-blame can send you into a negative spiral and either lead to emotional paralysis or acting-out behavior you may regret. On the other hand, to simply blame and bad-mouth your manager gets you nowhere either, and the possible aftermath of that behavior can deepen the chasm in which you find yourself. Pull back and look as objectively as possible at what **both** you and your manager might have done differently to reach a realistic and accurate appraisal of your efforts. This approach will generate solutions to rehabilitate your reputation. Remember, in the end, the only real control you have is over yourself—your own attitude and actions.

Figure out what went wrong

Try to pinpoint the source of the problem(s) that led your manager to give you an undeserved poor performance evaluation. You must be clear about the problem before you can fix it, **assuming it's fixable,** and you **want** to fix it. For example, if politics come into play, and you don't have the equipment or the will to join the game, you may want to look for a new playing field either inside or outside of the organization.

    Manager's Agenda and Politics. Try to determine your manager's agenda. Although this is one of the most important factors, it is often the most difficult to ascertain. Is your manager well meaning and just misguided in trying to help you improve performance? Is she trying to exert undue power and control over you? Is she a new person on the block and testing you, or is she trying to get rid of you so she can bring in her own team? Does she want to replace you with someone else who will take an approach to the job she prefers over yours? Is she playing favoritism and you're not a favorite? Is this payback for past confrontations or conflicts you've had with her?

Did a unique circumstance or incident taint your relationship with your manager? Did you fall prey to the "birds of a feather" syndrome—your boss dislikes or resents the people you associate with at work and projects their behavior or attitude onto you? Perhaps you got "gunny-sacked"? Your boss is carrying a grudge or dwelling on an unfavorable impression you made? Have you been "labeled"? Has your boss stereotyped you as "one of those _____ (aggressive feminists, big suits, troublemakers, etc.)"?

What techniques can you use to assess your manager's reason for giving you a poor evaluation?

> Review in your mind your past history with this manager. What repeated themes and patterns do you see that might give you insight to the problems we just listed?

> How does this manager treat others—your co-workers, his managers, business associates, and customers? Does he treat you differently than he does others? If he singles you out, could there be something in your behavior that triggers a negative reaction, even if you don't intend to? If he treats everyone the same, there is a personality characteristic you need to contend with.

> What is this manager's reputation with the organization? Can you glean clues to her reaction to you based on what others say about her? Take notice of others who seem to get along with her. What characteristics and behaviors does she respond to positively?

> Whom does he seem to prefer, favor, or associate with? Does he view you as part of the "in-group," "neutrally," or as an "outsider"? It may be that one of you is from Venus and the other one from Mars, regardless of gender. If you're coming from two different worlds, you have a serious problem.

New Boss, New Style, New Agenda. If your boss is new you may have simply suffered a time lapse; that is, there hasn't been sufficient time for the two of you to become familiar with each other's style, goals, perspective, and hot buttons. A little more time and some techniques suggested below might be just the tonic needed to cure your performance review ills.

> Within a 14-month period, Steve, a manager who worked for
> an office supply company, received the very best performance

review he'd ever had and the very worst. A new manager who'd been installed during a re-organization gave him the bad review. Steve figured out the fellow was new, somewhat unsure of his job, and eager to bring in his own people. Steve watched the new manager's style and listened for what he wanted. Then he went about his job doing his best, showing results, keeping a positive attitude, and reporting in the style the new manager preferred. As the manager became more comfortable with his position and confident that Steve could and would do the job, he began to view Steve as a valuable part of his team.

Clash of Styles. Do you and your boss have different ways of approaching the department's work? For example, is one of you a visionary who focuses on the big picture, whereas the other one is more concerned with the practicality of implementation? Instead of working as a complementary team you may butt heads as each of you struggles to execute the work according to your own comfortable style. If in fact you are meeting your goals and your manager is still unhappy with your performance, she may be focusing on "how" you do the job rather than the end results of the job.

A Break in the Communication Loop. Are you and your manager basically on the same page where it really counts, but trip over your lines when you try to communicate? Chapter 8 helps you analyze some of the kinks that occur in the communication loop, so look there for help if you determine this is a problem.

Misaligned Priorities. Do you and your manager hold different views of current priorities or how priorities should be handled? Does your manager think you are working on the wrong things, or putting too much emphasis on things she feels are less important? If the priorities and strategies set by your manager violate your basic values and make it impossible for you to agree to them, you most likely have an unfixable problem.

Diversity. Our workforce today is richly diverse with employees from all over the globe. Difficulties and misunderstandings are often due to differences in language, culture, customs, habits, or physical challenges, all of which can affect working and communication styles. We tend to be more critical of people who are different from ourselves, and managers as well as employees may be unaware they have fallen into this trap. Here's an example of how behavior that was normal for one person can appear abnormal to someone else and lead to workplace problems.

"I worked for along time in a busy lab in which we had to work closely together. There was one guy I didn't get along with. I was puzzled and frustrated by his hostility toward me. Finally one day he confronted me, demanding to know why I was "pushing" him whenever I wanted to talk to him. I was

shocked. Pushing?? I'm hearing impaired and have always touched people in a noisy place (like the lab) to get their attention. He misinterpreted my touch for a push. Once I explained that to him, we worked well together and became good friends. Communication was the key, and I was grateful he approached me about the problem. After that, I was much more careful about touching people to get their attention."

Develop a response

If you believe the situation is fixable, prepare a response to the items in the appraisal with which you disagree that you can present to your manager or others whom you may be meeting with. Be very specific in documenting as concretely as possible your good performance and the **results** you've achieved.

Review the process

Check your organization's policies and procedures for contesting a performance appraisal. Ideally, you'll be able to salvage the situation by having a productive conversation with your manager in which you arrive at a "meeting of the minds" and clarify misperceptions about your performance. However, if this doesn't work, you may have to follow the procedures to take your concerns to the next step.

A cautionary note about the end run: If you've exhausted all other possibilities, you may feel it's necessary to take your cause to your boss's boss, or higher. You may become the sacrificial lamb in this scenario, so carefully evaluate the political climate in your organization, the norms for making this kind of radical move, and what you have to gain. Seek the advice of a knowledgeable and politically savvy third party, someone objective who can counsel you about the advisability of the end run and the best way to handle it.

Clarify confusion, negotiate differences

Ideally you'll be able to meet with your manager to discuss, clarify, and gain consensus on the issues and the solutions if the problems stem from miscommunication, differences in style, or confusion over priorities.

Miscommunication. Check out Chapter 8 on feedback if you and your manager cross swords because you both constantly misinterpret and misconstrue information in conversations and repel each other with your different communication styles. Analyze your manager's preferred method of communication and consider modifying your communication style to help your manager "hear" and "understand" what you are really saying. It may be as simple as putting more information in writing, or taking a more casual or a more formal approach. You may want to explain and elaborate when you report, whereas your boss may want just the bottom-line facts. Give the boss what she wants. You can always elaborate later and vice versa.

Differences in Working Style. As with communication, differences in working style need to be discussed, clarified, and negotiated. Ideally you would meet each other halfway in an attempt to work as a complementary team rather than as adversaries. Determine how your manager approaches problems and projects and adjust your style or acknowledge his style sufficiently that you can meet on common ground. Let's say, for example, your manager's style is to gather all the information before making a decision and moving into action, whereas you like to take a little data and move quickly. You might want to present some data and then suggest to your boss that you begin working on one or two tasks while the other information is being gathered. And, of course, ask for recommendations as to what tasks those might be.

Many times, differences in working style are simply two roads to the same destination. In some cases, the battle to do it your way might not be worth it. Consider acquiescing to your boss's style, as long as the goals are met, and you don't have to rely on your weaker skills to do the job.

Misaligned Priorities. If your boss felt you didn't focus on the right priorities, meet with her to clarify what the goals and priorities are for you, the department, and the organization. Be sure to clearly articulate the results you achieved and the benefit to the organization, even if she disagrees about the target goals. Obviously, you and your manager need to align your goals.

Politics. Politics is always a gnarly subject. What are your options if your manager is playing politics and, despite your good performance, tries to move you out, diminish your role in the department, gives you the less important projects, or overrides your decisions?

If the game that's being played and the character of the players involved are consistent with your values, your challenge is to find out how to play the game and increase your stature with the players who already made the team. If the game is not compatible with your values you need to move elsewhere in the organization or find a position at another organization.

Trial run

Remember, the negotiations, compromises, and adjustments you and your manager attempt do not need to be cast in stone or a life sentence for either of you. Consider a trial run of a compromise or suggestion that either of you makes, and establish criteria and a timeline so you can both evaluate its success. You may find that you and your manager can forge a cooperative relationship incrementally as each of you learns to understand and trust the other.

The hare and the tortoise

As with the deserved bad performance review in the previous section, move quickly with a fast start out of the gate to fix the problem. Don't let a bad impression linger. By the same token, it may take a long, slow process of constant good performance and ongoing compromise to prove your worth and true self to your manager.

These techniques are golden if you have a reasonable manager whose agenda is to support his staff in getting the work of the organization done. If not, you have a much bigger career decision to make.

In summary, determine the ultimate agendas, and if the problem is solvable, demonstrate your successes, continue to exhibit good performance, clarify goals and expectations, and negotiate and compromise in communication and working style when you can.

Ultimately, what you want to demonstrate is that you are a great worker, you are willing to be flexible and cooperative, and your efforts and high-octane performance can make your manager look good!

If feedback, the lifeline of any productive relationship, is a challenge for you and your boss, come with us to Chapter 8, Dialogue: Giving and Getting Feedback. It's a lifesaver from your coach!

8

Dialogue:
Getting and Giving Feedback

The number one fear in America is NOT public speaking. It's FEEDBACK—Giving it and getting it. Productive career conversations depend heavily on a healthy feedback loop between employee and manager. Feedback is also a key ingredient for good teamwork. And that's what you and your boss are—a team.

Feedback is built into the once-a-year performance review process. Nurturing the feedback loop **all year** keeps both you and your manager on track, minimizes missteps, and builds a strong working relationship in which everyone wins.

Feedback exchanges are guideposts that keep you from wandering off center and signposts that point you in the right direction and keep you doing the right things.

Why is giving and getting feedback so difficult?

People are particularly reluctant to give negative, or constructive, criticism because, frankly, it's uncomfortable. No one likes to hurt people's feelings. But an incident occurred that reinforced for me the value of giving feedback.

> "I supervised an administrative assistant who also reported to two other people. She was a competent employee and a self-starter. But I wanted to give her constructive criticism on a project she was doing for me, because I knew with a little help she could do better. I was uncomfortable about it, however, because she worked so hard and threw so much of herself into the project. She came to me after receiving the feedback and gave me the most important message of my management career. She said, 'It's tough to get negative feedback on my work. But after my ego settles down, I feel good because your feedback helps me improve my work and develop skills. And when you compliment me, I know my work is good. Your feedback tells me you care about my work. The other supervisors just glance at my work, say OK, and pass it on. I don't feel they really value what I do'."

Giving feedback says you care about the person and his/her efforts. Soliciting feedback says you care about the person's advice, input, knowledge, and experience.

Review the following feedback checklists to help you assess your feedback attitudes and skills and those of your manager and co-workers. The more you understand about the feedback loop, the better you can use it as powerful tool. Productive feedback keeps a good career robust. If your career is ailing, a healing dose of feedback can be a healthy tonic.

Getting feedback from your manager, positive and negative, tells you:

❑ How you're doing.

❑ What progress you're making.

❑ What you do well.

❑ What you can do better.

❑ What you should keep doing.

❑ Resources that can help you.

❑ How you fit.

❑ If you're meeting expectations.

❑ You are a valued part of the team.

❑ What you need to do next.

❑ If you need to consider a career move.

Giving feedback to your manager demonstrates that you:

❑ Take initiative.

❑ Exert effort to work as a team with your manager.

❑ Care about developing your knowledge and skills.

❑ Acknowledge and care about your manager's advice.

❑ Want to make your manager's job easier.

People are reluctant to give feedback because they:

- ❑ Don't want to hurt people's feelings.

- ❑ Dread the reaction of the person getting negative feedback.

- ❑ Don't really want to deal with problems arising from feedback.

- ❑ Fear that they don't know how to deal with the employee's reaction to feedback.

- ❑ Don't feel skilled in giving feedback.

People often don't give positive feedback because they:

- ❑ Don't see its value.

- ❑ Aren't sensitive to the areas worthy of feedback.

- ❑ Feel they must reward the positive behavior described in the feedback.

- ❑ Aren't articulate about giving feedback.

- ❑ Feel it may be received as insincere and manipulative.

The willingness and ability to give feedback depends on an individual's:

- ❑ Personality and to what extent he or she is motivated by feedback.

- ❑ Value system: to what degree they value and appreciate feedback.

- ❑ Skill level in giving productive feedback.

- ❑ Experience and training in giving feedback.

- ❑ Personal painful or pleasurable experience in being the recipient of feedback.

Your Manager

A feedback star?

This chapter will be a breeze for those of you who have managers who give plentiful and skilled feedback. If your manager is a feedback artist, observe him or her closely, and use the list on the previous page to determine why he is skillful. You can learn a great deal from a good role model.

Still playing off Broadway?

Do you have a boss who does not give feedback or is less than artful at doing it? If so, the responsibility for fostering two-way feedback falls in your court. It's in your best interest to be courageous and clever in giving and getting feedback. If you'd like to improve your feedback skills, start here with Chapter 8. As we did in Chapters 6 and 7, we'll ply you with examples and put words in your mouth with handy feedback tips and scripts.

You and Your Manager: An Historical Perspective

Before you begin to formulate scripts for giving and soliciting feedback, review the working relationship you've had with your manager. This will surface ideas, thoughts, and reactions that will be pertinent as you initiate the feedback loop and engage your manager in the feedback process. This quick review will make it easier for you to formulate how you want to approach your manager and what you want to say. The work you did in Chapter 4, The Stage Set, will help you with this exercise.

In what ways has your manager helped to make your job easier?
(For example: gives clear directions, tells what's expected, keeps you informed)

_____

_____

_____

_____

_____

In what ways has your manager helped your career?
(For example: provides resources, training, coaches you in the job skills)

_____

_____

_____

_____

Has your manager made your job more difficult? If so, how?
(For example: changes goals, micro-manages, won't make timely decisions)

_____

_____

_____

_____

Do you and your boss have compatible work and communication styles? If compatible, how?
(For example: manager works on the big picture; you work on details)

_____

_____

_____

_____

_____

Do you and your boss have incompatible work and communication styles? If so, what are they?
(For example: manager likes written communication, you prefer face-to-face; or manager focuses on emotions and feelings, you prefer objectivity and bottom line)

_____

_____

_____

_____

_____

How can you and your boss modify styles to be more compatible?
(For example: you write down communication first, then meet face-to-face)

_____

_____

_____

_____

_____

What could your manager do to support your work efforts?
(For example: more training, more feedback, get needed resources)

_____

_____

_____

_____

_____

Your responses to these questions will help you generate information you want to solicit and give in feedback sessions.

Tips to make your feedback encounters successful

1. Pick the right time and place to solicit or deliver feedback
Chasing down the hall after your boss who is late for an appointment (heaven forbid you should take a header) or approaching your boss after a tense meeting are not good times to get objective feedback. Timing and context are critical elements in productive feedback sessions. Obviously, the performance review is an ideal time to solicit feedback, since that's one of its main purposes, but be alert to other opportunities throughout the year to give and get feedback, and pick your time and place carefully.

2. Be a good scout: PREPARE
Think through what you want to say and how you want to say it. Write scripts if you need to.

3. Pick your battles
If you have a list of sensitive issues, either for soliciting or giving feedback, pick the most important ones to tackle first. Don't hit your manager with both barrels, particularly if the feedback you have is negative.

4. Be POSITIVE even when giving negative feedback
Be positive and upbeat about the future and the chance of success. For example, it's better to say "I work more productively when you give me clear goals," versus "I don't like it when you don't give me clear goals."

5. Emphasize the benefit to the organization
For example, in soliciting feedback, ask, "In what other ways could I develop my career that benefits the organization and makes me a more satisfied and productive worker?" Or in giving feedback, say, "If you give me the bigger picture of what's happening, I can adjust my work to fit in better with what the other departments need."

6. Stay cool—like that cucumber
Use feedback sessions as a positive way to make progress, not a soapbox for venting pent-up anger or frustration. Don't let emotions rule. Stay objective, and focus on the end goal and what you really want. Don't fall into the "It-feels-so-good-to-dump" trap.

Now let's start with feedback you'd like to receive.

How to Solicit Feedback From Your Manager

Often we fall into the trap of thinking that the manager is in sole control of feedback. Many managers would do handsprings if their employees would assist with this important and difficult process. You can assist, and here's how to do it.

Watch out! Here comes your manager somersaulting down the hall. She's probably happy, so chances are it's a good time to get her attention—that is after she's cooled down and caught her breath. Timing is critical to success.

The most important feedback from your manager falls into four main categories: 1) your progress on projects and tasks, 2) goals, 3) your personal development, and 4) you and your manager's working relationship. Try on the questions we've tucked under each of these categories. Find the ones that work for you.

1. Soliciting feedback about projects and tasks completed or in progress

In progress

- Do my solutions/approaches seem realistic?

- Do you see other strategies I can use to complete this project?

- Could I have done (or can I do) anything differently or better?

- Are there other resources I might have used (or can use)?

- Do you feel my time frame is realistic?

- Have you supervised other projects like this? How did they go?

Completed

- Do you see other benefits (aside from the ones I've listed) for the organization from work I've accomplished?

- Has the project/task I've accomplished met or exceeded your expectations?

- What, if anything, might I have done better or differently?

2. Soliciting feedback about goals and expectations

- Do my stated goals/expectations seem realistic?

- Are they related to the primary needs and goals of our department/the organization?

- Are my time frames realistic?

- Can you suggest other strategies or resources I can use to implement my goals and expectations?

3. Soliciting feedback about your growth and development

- Are my development goals in line with the organization's needs?

- Are they an accurate reflection of the areas I need to develop?

- What would you add to this list?

- Have I been progressing at a rate you would expect?

- Can you add to my ideas as to ways to continue to grow and develop?

- What would it take for me to attain a position in _____?

4. Soliciting feedback about the working relationship you have with your manager

- Are there ways I could do a better job of communicating to you?

- What do you feel is the best way to tackle a problem/project?

- What do you think about my style in _____ if I produce the result you want?

- Is there a way we could agree or compromise on our differences in _____?

- How can I be a better support to your style and way of doing things?

- What can I do to make your job easier?

How to Give Feedback to Your Manager

Now we get to the dicey part of the process—how to tell your manager what you need to be a satisfied and productive employee. Think of it as "helping your manager help you." Start with the positive things your manager does to make your job easier and more successful. Then follow with diplomatic statements and questions that get into the areas that cause you problems. Try these on for size.

I appreciated the way you _____. It made it much easier for me to complete that part of the assignment.

Thank you for _____. It was a real help on the _____.

It helped that you said_____. I got the picture of what was needed.

What I struggle with most is_____. It would help me if you could_____.

Could you put critical "to do's" in writing so it's easier for us to track?

Can we meet for a few minutes regularly to go over priorities? I work better when I can clearly see the priorities and end goal.

It would help if you would explain the bigger picture and show me how what I do relates to other activities in the department/ division/organization.

Are there other resources or people who can help with my part of this project?

Specifics are very helpful to me on a project of this size. Could you be more specific about what you want done and when?

Would you share with me the expectations and criteria for this project?

As this project moves forward, it would be invaluable for me to know from you what is going well, what has been done correctly, and what we can do differently.

I learn from knowing what I do right as well as what I do wrong. Would you share both with me?

I'm committed to this new assignment, but my current workload gives me only 15 minutes a day to work on it. I would like to review some options with you and see what ideas you have about how I can get more time to devote to this project.

I can see we're running behind on this assignment. I think I could save us some time if I _____, if you _____, if we_____.

Handling Feedback on Projects That Hit a Bump

There's another topic that needs special attention in any discussion about work performance, progress, and goals—how do you handle projects in trouble?

Every project or task has its challenges. It's not only avoiding problems that's the issue in performance, but how you deal with them when they inevitably do surface.

This format allows you to communicate the obstacles you're facing in a systematic and effective manner and shows how YOU are being proactive and resourceful in overcoming the obstacles, solving the problem, salvaging the project, and moving on.

1. I have already completed these parts of the project:

_____

_____

_____

_____

2. The incomplete phase of the project is:

_____

_____

_____

3. Key obstacles and problems that stand in the way are:

_____

_____

_____

4. This is what I'm doing to solve the problem:

_____

_____

_____

_____

5. Here's a list of help and resources needed in order to move this project along:

_____

_____

_____

_____

6. By putting the above action items in place, the project can be completed by:

_____

_____

_____

_____

Share and Explore Ideas

A primary responsibility of a manager is to groom and grow people. The more you help your manager do this, the more your manager can help you. It's a win-win cycle of mutual help and support. When preparing for formal and informal career conversations, include in that preparation ideas and suggestions you have for your own growth and development. Then solicit additional help and resources from your manager. The resourcefulness you exhibit will inspire your manager to help you in this endeavor.

The work you've done in the previous chapters has laid the groundwork. Now, do some creative thinking and come up with ideas and suggestions for your growth and development, and SHARE them with your manager. Here are some words and phrases you can use.

I would like to take a class on _____ that would help me improve my (skills, knowledge of _____.

Here is a list of places that offer this class. Do you have other suggestions? I've looked into education reimbursement and _____.

I'm going to talk to _____ in our _____ department to find out more about how we _____. I would appreciate your ideas on questions I should ask that would help our department and me.

I'd like to attend the _____ industry association because it would help me (do my job better, help on a project, meet other professionals, etc.). Do you have any feedback about the group and what else I might have to gain by attending? Is there room in our budget to reimburse my costs?

I've heard about an organization-wide committee looking at employee relations programs. How do they select employees for the committee and what are my chances of being selected?

I was looking in our course catalog and found three possible workshops that are of interest to me. Which of these do you think would be best for me to take?

I want to subscribe to a good _____ publication. I'm considering _____ or _____. Do you have an opinion or more suggestions?

In summary, managers are people. (Now that's a profound statement!) They come to the workplace with a variety of different personalities, backgrounds, skills, emotional states, egos, and agendas. Some of them were in positions just like yours—yesterday. The degree of success you experience in the feedback process will depend in great part on your attitude going in and on your manager's own agenda. Hopefully your agendas are the same, basically to work together toward the same end. What a TEAM!

If your manager's attitude and intentions are in the right place, but he or she is immobilized by fear or a lack of feedback skills, your manager, most likely, will appear unapproachable and uncooperative, but in fact will appreciate and reward your efforts. Putting energy, skills, and creativity into feedback will reap rewards, no matter the state or condition of management. You will win because you know what you want and what you need. You'll be proactive in managing your career. And, you'll have a better idea of where you stand; remember, no feedback from your manager is feedback.

Curtain Call

As the final curtain descends on this book, you, the scriptwriter, director, and star performer, deserve a curtain call—so take a bow. You've worked diligently to gather your basic career information, understand your company's needs, determine career goals, prepare for performance reviews and career conversations, solicit feedback, and weave engaging stories to captivate your audience.

The purpose of this book on performance reviews and career conversations has been to put you in control as you make career decisions and walk onstage in any arena. Clients who've had interview training tell us they relish interviewing after they've been coached because they are eager to use their newfound ability to communicate their skills and achievements. They feel a sense of accomplishment and a new confidence because they have conquered a once-daunting task.

Our goal is the same—to have you primed and pumped for your performance review, secure in the knowledge that you know what you want, know what you've got, and are equipped with the scripts and stories to communicate it.

Armed with the insight, techniques, and enthusiasm for holding winning performance reviews and career conversations, you can break through any fear or reluctance you may feel toward the appraisal process and burst onto the stage to play your leading role!

Here's to a standing ovation!

Order Form

List the titles or send this form—complete with your name, address, and payment—to:

Impact Publications

9104 Manassas Drive, Suite N, Manassas Park, VA 20111-5211
Tel. 1.800.361.1055 (orders only) • 703.361.7300 • Fax 703.335.9486
Quick and easy online ordering: www.impactpublications.com
e-mail: info@impactpublications.com

Featured Resources

BOOKS AND SPECIALS

____	101 Best Resumes for Grads	$11.95 _____
____	300 Best Jobs Without a College Degree	$16.95 _____
____	America's Top Jobs for People...Degrees	$15.95 _____
____	Barron's Profiles of American Colleges	$26.95 _____
____	Career Counselor's Handbook	$17.95 _____
____	Colleges With Programs for...Disabilities	$29.95 _____
____	Discover the Best Jobs for You	$15.95 _____
____	Discover What You're Best At	$14.00 _____
____	GED Success	$16.95 _____
____	High Impact Resumes and Letters	$19.95 _____
____	High-Stakes Test Series	$65.95 _____
____	No One Will Hire Me!	$13.95 _____
____	Occupational Outlook Handbook	$16.95/21.95 _____
____	Peterson's Complete Guide to Colleges	$49.95 _____
____	Peterson's Complete Guide to Financial Aid	$49.95 _____
____	Right Words at the Right Time	$25.00 _____
____	Self Matters	$25.00 _____
____	Seven Habits of Highly Effective People	$14.00 _____
____	Ten Things I Wish I'd Known Before I Went...	$19.95 _____
____	Who Moved My Cheese?	$19.95 _____
____	Words Can Heal Handbook	$9.95 _____

VIDEOS

____	10 Keys to Success for At-Risk Students	$89.00 _____
____	10 Ways to Boost Low Self-Esteem	$89.00 _____
____	50 Best Jobs for the 21st Century Series	$545.00 _____
____	Anger, Temper Tantrums, and Violent Emotions	$89.00 _____
____	Build a Network for Work and Life	$149.00 _____
____	Careers in Criminal Justice	$79.95 _____
____	College Not Required for Great Jobs	$189.00 _____
____	Complete Job Application	$149.00 _____
____	Coping With Fighters, Bullies...Troublemakers	$89.00 _____
____	Getting Along With Others	$89.00 _____
____	Make a Good First Impression	$129.00 _____
____	Resisting Pressure to Join Gangs	$89.00 _____
____	Seizing the Job Interview	$79.00 _____
____	Stressproofing Teens for Tough Times	$89.00 _____
____	Teen Guide to Effective Study Skills	$89.00 _____
____	Teen Guide to Surviving Divorce	$89.00 _____
____	Think Small	$149.00 _____
____	Tips & Techniques to Improve Your...Image	$98.00 _____
____	What Every Teen Must Know About...Tobacco	$89.00 _____
____	Why Should I Hire You?	$129.00 _____

New and Recently Published

CAREER PREP

____	25 Jobs That Have it All	$12.95 _____
____	50 Cutting Edge Jobs	$15.95 _____
____	101 Dynamite Answers to Interview Questions	$12.95 _____
____	101 Dynamite Questions to Ask...Interview	$13.95 _____
____	101 Secrets of Highly Effective Speakers	$15.95/31.95 _____
____	150 Great Tech Prep Careers	$29.95 _____
____	201 Dynamite Job Search Letters	$19.95 _____
____	250 Job Interview Questions You'll...Asked	$9.95 _____
____	America's Fastest Growing Jobs	$15.95 _____
____	America's Top Internet Job Sites	$19.95 _____
____	America's Top Jobs Series	$157.95 _____
____	Back Door Guide to Short-Term...Adventures	$21.95 _____
____	Beyond Business Casual	$14.99 _____
____	Big Red Book of Resumes	$16.95 _____
____	Building Your Career Portfolio	$13.99 _____

____	But What if I Don't Want to Go to College	$12.95	_____
____	Career Compass	$20.95	_____
____	Career Opportunities in Computers...	$18.95	_____
____	Career Tests	$12.95	_____
____	Careers in Criminology	$16.95	_____
____	Change Your Job, Change Your Life	$17.95	_____
____	Connecting With Success	$20.95	_____
____	Creating Your High School Resume...Portfolio	$29.95	_____
____	Dancing Naked	$14.95	_____
____	Directory of Websites for International Jobs	$19.95	_____
____	Dynamite Salary Negotiations	$15.95	_____
____	e-Resumes	$11.95	_____
____	Eat That Frog!	$19.95	_____
____	Encyclopedia of Careers and...Guidance	$159.95	_____
____	Everything Job Finding Series	$48.95	_____
____	Expert Resume Series	$48.95	_____
____	Foot in the Door	$14.95	_____
____	Free and Inexpensive Career Materials	$19.95	_____
____	Great Careers in Two Years	$19.95	_____
____	Habit Busting	$13.00	_____
____	High-Tech Careers for Low-Tech People	$14.95	_____
____	How Rude!	$19.95	_____
____	How to Be a Star at Work	$12.00	_____
____	How to Get a Job and Keep It	$16.95	_____
____	How to Make People Like You in...Less	$14.95	_____
____	How to Work a Room	$14.00	_____
____	If Life Is a Game, These Are the Rules	$15.00	_____
____	If Success Is a Game, These Are the Rules	$17.50	_____
____	Improvise This!	$22.95	_____
____	Inside Secrets to Finding a Career in Travel	$14.95	_____
____	International Job Finder	$19.95	_____
____	Interview for Success	$15.95	_____
____	Interview Rehearsal Book	$12.00	_____
____	Job Search Handbook for People...Disabilities	$16.95	_____
____	Jobs for Smart Dummies Series	$109.95	_____
____	Knock 'Em Dead	$12.95	_____
____	Life Strategies	$21.95	_____
____	Major in Success	$12.95	_____
____	Make Your Contacts Count	$14.95	_____
____	Masters of Networking	$16.95	_____
____	Maximum Success	$24.95	_____
____	Resumes, Cover Letters, and Portfolios	$98.00	_____
____	Ten Commandments of Resumes	$79.95	_____
____	Web Resumes	$89.00	_____
____	Your Resume	$99.00	_____

Interview Videos

____	Common Mistakes People Make in Interviews	$79.95	_____
____	Exceptional Interviewing Tips	$79.00	_____
____	Extraordinary Answers to Common Interview...	$79.95	_____
____	Extreme Interview	$69.00	_____
____	Interview Tips From a Recruiter	$98.00	_____
____	Interviews That Win Jobs	$99.00	_____
____	Job Search	$150.00	_____
____	Make the Interview Count	$98.00	_____
____	Quick Interview Video	$149.00	_____
____	Quick Salary Negotiation Video	$149.00	_____
____	Secrets to Job Fair Success	$99.00	_____
____	Seizing the Job Interview	$79.00	_____
____	Why Should I Hire You?	$129.00	_____

Finding Your First Job Videos

____	Best 101/4 Tips for Finding Your First Job	$98.00	_____
____	You DO Have Experience!	$149.00	_____
____	Your First Resume and Interview	$89.95	_____

Job Keeping and Advancement Videos 60-61

____	Accepting the Challenge	$89.00	_____
____	An Introduction to the Rules of Work	$98.00	_____
____	Best 101/4 Tips for Awesome Work Habits	$98.00	_____
____	Eight Easy Ways to Lose a Job	$129.00	_____
____	Employer's Expectations	$95.00	_____

____	Exceptional Employee	$79.00 ____
____	How to Be a Success at Work Video Series	$329.00 ____
____	Job Survival Kit	$79.95 ____
____	Job Survival Skills	$129.00 ____
____	Life After High School	$89.00 ____
____	Necessary Skills for the Workplace	$98.00 ____
____	Social Skills at Work	$89.00 ____
____	Success in the Job World Video Series	$719.00 ____
____	Work Habits for the Beginner	$125.00 ____
____	Work Maturity Skills Video Series	$799.00 ____
____	Work Skills and Habits for Job Success	$69.00 ____
____	Workplace Issues Video Series	$449.00 ____

Software

____	12 Biggest Mistakes Job Hunters...Make	$149.95 ____
____	Ace the Interview	$99.00 ____
____	CareerExplorer CD-ROM	$295.00 ____
____	CareerOINK	$____ ____
____	CD-ROM Version of the OOH	$399.00 ____
____	Healthy Lifestyles CD Series	$____ ____
____	Improved Career Decision Making...CD-ROM	$89.95 ____
____	Interview Skills for the Future CD-ROM	$199.00 ____
____	JIST's Multimedia OOH	$____ ____
____	Job Browser Pro 1.2	$295.00 ____
____	Job Search CD Series	$____ ____
____	Job Search Skills for the 21st Century	$199.00 ____
____	Job Survival CD Series	$____ ____
____	Job World Issues CD Series	$____ ____
____	Multimedia Career Center	$385.00 ____
____	Multimedia Career Path CD-ROM	$89.95 ____
____	Multimedia Career Pathway Assessment...	$199.00 ____
____	Multimedia Occupational GOE Assessment...	$449.00 ____
____	Multimedia Personal Development CD-ROM...	$450.00 ____
____	Multimedia Right Resume Writer	$199.00 ____
____	School-to-Work Career Center	$385.00 ____
____	So...What Are You Going to Do With...Series	$1,950.00 ____
____	Young Person's Electronic Occupational...CD	$____ ____

SUBTOTAL ____

Virginia residents (4% sales tax) ... ____

Shipping/handling: $5 for first item ... ____

plus following percentages when SUBTOTAL is:

- $10-$99—multiply subtotal by 8% ... ____
- $100-$999—multiply subtotal by 7% ... ____
- $1,000-$4,999—multiply subtotal by 6% ... ____
- Over $5,000—multiply subtotal by 5% ... ____
- If shipped outside Continental US, add another 5% ... ____

Total Enclosed ____

Individuals must prepay as follows:
- Check • Money Order enclosed for: $_____

- Visa • MC • AmEx • Discover for: $_____ Card # _____ Exp:____/____

Signature_____

Approved Organizations may submit official (signed) purchase orders for net 30-day payment terms:

- Purchase Order enclosed: # _____ Signature_____

Billing Information:
Name:

Address:

Telephone:

Email:

Ship To (Please specify a street delivery address):
Name:

Address:

Telephone:

Keep in Touch . . .
On the Web!

www.impactpublications.com
www.winningthejob.com
www.contentforcareers.com
www.ishoparoundtheworld.com
www.contentfortravel.com